The Sinking of the Titanic

Thomas Streissguth, *Book Editor*

Daniel Leone, *Publisher*
Bonnie Szumski, *Editorial Director*
Scott Barbour, *Managing Editor*

AT ISSUE IN HISTORY

Greenhaven Press, Inc.
San Diego, California

No part of this book may be reproduced or used in any form or by any means, electrical, mechanical, or otherwise, including, but not limited to, photocopy, recording, or any information storage and retrieval system, without prior written permission from the publisher.

Library of Congress Cataloging-in-Publication Data

The sinking of the Titanic / Thomas Streissguth, book editor.
    p.   cm. — (At issue in history)
  Includes bibliographical references and index.
  ISBN 0-7377-0824-7 (pbk. : alk. paper)—
ISBN 0-7377-0825-5 (lib. bdg. : alk. paper)
   1. Titanic (Steamship) 2. Shipwrecks—North Atlantic Ocean. I. Streissguth, Thomas, 1958– II. Series.

G530.T6 S55 2002
910'.91634—dc21
2001033896

Cover photo: © Bettmann/Corbis

© 2002 by Greenhaven Press, Inc., PO Box 289009,
San Diego, CA 92198-9009

Printed in the U.S.A.

Every effort has been made to trace owners of copyrighted material.

LIBRARY
John Bowne High School
63-25 Main Street
Flushing, N.Y. 11367

Contents

Foreword   8

Introduction   10

Chapter 1: Early Accounts and Inquiries

1. The *Hampshire Chronicle* Reports the Wreck of the *Titanic by the* Hampshire Chronicle   17

   The new medium of wireless telegraphy allowed the print media to quickly deliver the news of the *Titanic*'s sinking. A local paper gives the first sketchy reports of the disaster to readers in Southampton, the English home port of the R.M.S. *Titanic*.

2. A Tragedy Caused by Misplaced Confidence *by the* New York Sun   23

   Speculation about the cause of the *Titanic* disaster filled the pages of daily newspapers for many weeks after the sinking. This *New York Sun* article suggests that the collision with the iceberg occurred because the *Titanic*'s captain traveled at dangerously high speeds due to his confidence that the ship was unsinkable.

3. The *Titanic*'s Crew Ineptly Handled the Ship's Lifeboats *by Marshall Everett*   26

   The *Titanic*'s crew was not properly trained in deployment of the ship's lifeboats. When tragedy struck, many lives were lost because the crew handled the lifeboats poorly.

4. Captain Smith's Indifference to Danger Contributed to the Tragedy *by William Alden Smith*   29

   An uproar took place after the *Titanic*'s sinking, as the public demanded explanations and scapegoats. On May 28, 1912, at the conclusion of the U.S. Senate's official inquiry into the disaster, Senator William Alden Smith, the inquiry chairman, criticized the ship's captain for failing to proceed with due caution when confronted with the danger of floating ice.

5. The *Titanic*'s Navigators Are Found Negligent
   by Geoffrey Marcus   38
   In 1913, Thomas Ryan, an Irish farmer who had lost a son on the *Titanic*, sued the owners of the *Titanic* for negligence in civil court. The jury found the *Titanic*'s navigators guilty of negligence for traveling at an unsafe speed through icy waters.

6. New Instructions for White Star Line Captains
   by White Star Line   50
   The White Star Line grew safety-conscious after the sinking of its luxurious flagship. New instructions delivered to the company's captains emphasized the new policy.

Chapter 2: The *Titanic* and the *Californian*

1. The Failures of the *Californian*'s Captain and Crew *by C.V. Groves*   53
   The Leyland freighter *Californian* stood motionless only ten miles from the *Titanic*'s position throughout the sinking. One of the ship's officers recounts the events of that night and attempts to solve some of the mysteries regarding the *Californian*'s inaction.

2. The Captain of the *Californian* Defends Himself
   by Stanley Lord   61
   Captain Stanley Lord spent a lifetime explaining and defending his actions as commander of the *Californian* on the night of April 14, 1912. In this affidavit, he defends himself and advances the theory that the *Californian* was much farther from the *Titanic* that night than is commonly supposed.

3. The Captain of the *Californian* May Have Acted Reasonably *by Stephen Cox*   73
   It was the opinion of many that the actions of First Officer Murdoch aboard the *Titanic*, and of Captain Lord aboard the *Californian*, doomed the *Titanic* and fifteen hundred of its passengers and crew. In this analysis, author Stephen Cox finds those actions to have been prudent, logical, and extremely unlucky.

Chapter 3: Modern Perspectives on the Sinking of the *Titanic*

1. The *Titanic*'s Reckless Captain *by Michael Davie*   80
   This author portrays the *Titanic*'s captain, Edward J. Smith, as a capable and experienced seaman, but one who may have suffered from the weakness of overconfidence—an often fatal attribute at sea.

2. The *Titanic* and Its Times: When Accountants Ruled the Waves *by Roy Brander*   88
   Author Roy Brander argues that there was much more to the *Titanic* disaster than a fatal brush against an iceberg. Partly to blame was the corporate competition between the White Star Line and other commercial shipping companies.

3. Brittle Steel May Have Contributed to the *Titanic*'s Sinking *by Robert Gannon*   95
   Scientists, engineers, and historians have long debated the facts surrounding the *Titanic*'s sinking. The discovery of the ship's remains in 1985, and the recovery of hull fragments from the sea bottom, gave rise to the new "brittle steel" theory, in which the ship's material is partially blamed for the extensive damage done by the iceberg.

4. Captain Smith Inadvertently Sank the *Titanic* *by David G. Brown*   105
   The popular image of the *Titanic*'s starboard bow scraping the iceberg is not only false, but impossible, according to this analysis. The ship must have grounded on top of the iceberg, while Captain Smith's orders to restart the ship's engines and make for Halifax after the collision actually brought about the sinking.

For Further Research   124

Index   125

Foreword

Historian Robert Weiss defines history simply as "a record and interpretation of past events." Both elements—record and interpretation—are necessary, Weiss argues.

> Names, dates, places, and events are the essence of history. But historical writing is not a compendium of facts. It consists of facts placed in a sequence to tell a connected story. A work of history is not merely a story, however. It also must analyze what happened and *why*—that is, it must interpret the past for the reader.

For example, the events of December 7, 1941, that led President Franklin D. Roosevelt to call it "a date which will live in infamy" are fairly well known and straightforward. A force of Japanese planes and submarines launched a torpedo and bombing attack on American military targets in Pearl Harbor, Hawaii. The surprise assault sank five battleships, disabled or sank fourteen additional ships, and left almost twenty-four hundred American soldiers and sailors dead. On the following day, the United States formally entered World War II when Congress declared war on Japan.

These facts and consequences were almost immediately communicated to the American people who heard reports about Pearl Harbor and President Roosevelt's response on the radio. All realized that this was an important and pivotal event in American and world history. Yet the news from Pearl Harbor raised many unanswered questions. Why did Japan decide to launch such an offensive? Why were the attackers so successful in catching America by surprise? What did the attack reveal about the two nations, their people, and their leadership? What were its causes, and what were its effects? Political leaders, academic historians, and students look to learn the basic facts of historical events and to read the intepretations of these events by many different sources, both primary and secondary, in order to develop a more complete picture of the event in a historical context.

In the case of Pearl Harbor, several important questions surrounding the event remain in dispute, most notably the role of President Roosevelt. Some historians have blamed his policies for deliberately provoking Japan to attack in order to propel America into World War II; a few have gone so far as to accuse him of knowing of the impending attack but not informing others. Other historians, examining the same event, have exonerated the president of such charges, arguing that the historical evidence does not support such a theory.

The Greenhaven At Issue in History series recognizes that many important historical events have been interpreted differently and in some cases remain shrouded in controversy. Each volume features a collection of articles that focus on a topic that has sparked controversy among eyewitnesses, contemporary observers, and historians. An introductory essay sets the stage for each topic by presenting background and context. Several chapters then examine different facets of the subject at hand with readings chosen for their diversity of opinion. Each selection is preceded by a summary of the author's main points and conclusions. A bibliography is included for those students interested in pursuing further research. An annotated table of contents and thorough index help readers to quickly locate material of interest. Taken together, the contents of each of the volumes in the Greenhaven At Issue in History series will help students become more discriminating and thoughtful readers of history.

Introduction

At 2:20 A.M. on the morning of April 15, 1912, the R.M.S. *Titanic*, a passenger liner of forty-six thousand gross tons belonging to the White Star Line, sank in the North Atlantic Ocean about two hours and forty minutes after striking an iceberg that lay in its path. More than fifteen hundred passengers and crew perished. Later that morning, the news of the tragedy spread around the world through the medium of wireless telegraphic communication. As the *Hampshire Chronicle* of Southampton, the *Titanic*'s home port, described it, the wreck was "a terrible disaster, unparalleled in the records of the sea."[1]

Not only had the *Titanic* been the largest, most up-to-date, and most luxurious passenger liner afloat, it had been sailing its maiden voyage along the busiest sea lanes in the world. The ship had been carrying wealthy British and American aristocrats in high style; among their company were Thomas Andrews, the ship's designer, and J. Bruce Ismay, managing director of the White Star Line. There were second-class passengers enjoying slightly lesser comforts, as well as immigrants confined to the spare third-class accommodations on the lower decks. It would be several days before a list of the survivors could be published; in the meantime, as the ship carrying the survivors made its way to New York, the worried public spread its many rumors about exactly how and why the sinking had occurred—a question that still burns among historians, maritime engineers, and the deep-sea archaeologists that discovered the *Titanic*'s remains in 1985.

Capturing the Public's Imagination

Something about the *Titanic* disaster gripped the imagination and provoked the wonder of all who heard or read of it. There seemed to be a supernatural hand at work in the sudden destruction, at the light touch of a passing iceberg, of such an immense, sturdy, and reputedly "unsinkable" marvel of modern shipping. The *Titanic* had been designed to assure passengers, officers, and crew that it was the very latest ship afloat, the safest and most reliable means of transportation in the world. Confidence in the ship ran so high that, by direction of the White Star management, lifeboats had only been provided for less than one-half of the ship's full complement of passengers in order to provide more space for those wishing to promenade on the liner's upper decks.

Yet instead of carrying its passengers safely and luxuriously to New York, the *Titanic* sailed a little over thirty-two hundred miles, into the dead calm of the evening of April 14, struck an iceberg, and sank by the bow. The collision itself was felt only as a slight jarring within the ship, as reported by passenger Lawrence Beesley:

> There came what seemed to me nothing more than an extra heave of the engines and a more than usually obvious dancing motion of the mattress on which I sat. Nothing more than that—no sound of a crash or anything else: no sense of shock, no jar that felt like one heavy body meeting another.[2]

Beesley and others dismissed the light jarring and returned to their sleep, if awakened, or to the ordinary pursuits of a Sunday evening at sea. But shortly after midnight, with the ship beginning to dip into the sea, the crew raised the alarm belowdecks, and a scramble for the lifeboats began. The crew manned their boat stations, careful to admit women and children first, followed by men only after no

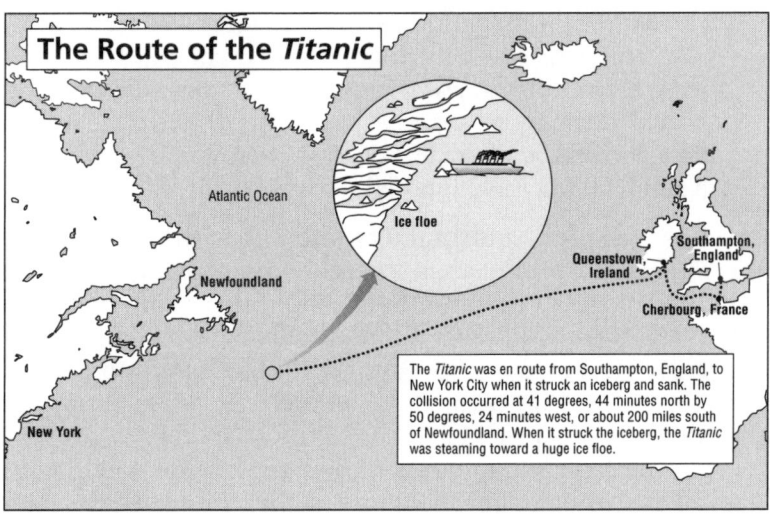

women and children could be found to take up available space. Within the hour, the boat deck was filled with worried passengers and rushing crew members; fragile lifeboats were being lowered into the water, and the ship's officers were peparing themselves for the fate they now knew was in store: the death of the *Titanic*. While the ship's two radiomen frantically sent out calls for assistance, officers touched off white distress rockets from the deck, praying that somewhere along this busy sea track a ship was close enough to reach their position before the *Titanic* foundered. These officers knew, from long experience, that nature and the sea can harshly punish human overconfidence.

A Sinkable Ship

The *Titanic*'s hull had been designed with a series of sixteen watertight compartments, separated by massive iron bulkheads running longitudinally across the lower half of the ship. In case of a hull breach—as a result of the ship hitting an object, a reef, or another ship—the officer in comand could order the watertight doors closed, allowing the compartment filling with water to be sealed off from its neighbors. The design was the most advanced of its kind in the world; the "watertight" design of the individual compartments gave rise to the myth that the entire ship was "watertight" as well. As Senator William Alden Smith pronounced at the official Senate inquiry into the disaster:

> Builders of renown had launched her on the billows with confident assurance of her strength, while every port rang with praise for their achievement. . . . In the construction of the *Titanic* no limit of cost circumscribed their endeavor, and when this vessel took its place at the head of the line every modern improvement in shipbuilding was supposed to have been realized.[3]

The designers and builders knew that there remained the remote possibility that several compartments could be breached at the same time. In addition, if the ship began to sink by the bow, any water filling the front of the ship could move over the tops of the watertight bulkheads and toward the stern. This, unfortunately, was exactly what happened on the night of April 14.

Yet the fault for the *Titanic* disaster lay not solely with natural causes or engineering oversights. Human error and simple bad luck also contributed to the tragedy. Captain Edward J. Smith, the most experienced officer in the White Star fleet, and the best-paid sailor in the world, had his ship proceeding at full steam despite the numerous ice warnings he had received the previous afternoon. The calm, waveless, and moonless night made it difficult for the ship's lookouts to spot objects at a distance—especially as they happened not to have their binoculars at hand that night. They did spot the iceberg before the collision—but at the precise moment when turning the vessel sharply away from it allowed the berg to hit the *Titanic* a glancing, fatal blow. If the lookouts had raised the alarm a few seconds earlier, the ship might have avoided the iceberg altogether; a few seconds later, and the *Titanic* would have hit the berg head-on, destroying its bow but allowing the watertight compartments to do their job and prevent the ship from sinking.

The *Californian* and the *Carpathia*

It is believed that the Leyland freighter *Californian* was about ten miles away from the *Titanic* at the time it sank. Much controversy has surrounded the actions of the *Californian*'s captain, Stanley Lord, on that fateful night. The crew of the *Titanic* saw the *Californian* and attempted to signal the ship with a Morse lamp and by firing eight flares. The crew aboard the *Californian* saw the flares and reported this sighting to Lord. However, Lord was apparently not convinced that the flares were distress signals, perhaps believing them to be part of some kind of late-night celebration.

Like most modern ships, the *Californian* did carry wireless equipment on board, as well as an operator who knew how to use it. Unfortunately, the set had just been turned off for the night as the *Titanic* sent out its first distress calls and prepared its rockets for launching. Captain Lord may have realized the import of the rockets and, weighing the risk to his own ship, decided to do nothing rather than attempt a passage through the icefield to investigate. As *Titanic* historian Stephen Cox makes the point in his book *The Titanic Story*:

> It is possible that Lord was hesitant to rouse his wireless operator because he did not want to confirm the fact that another vessel was in distress and find himself obligated to do something about it. He weighed the risks, both from ice and from moral responsibility, and he tried to reduce them to the lowest possible level.[4]

The *Titanic*'s lifeboats saved about 720 passengers and crew members from death by exposure and drowning.[5] The boats wandered aimlessly for a few hours until the Cunard liner *Carpathia* arrived to pluck them from the sea. Several hundred bodies were recovered, as were fragments of deck chairs, empty lifebelts, and smaller debris. The rest of the Titanic had disappeared.

Laying the Blame

For many decades after the *Titanic* tragedy, officials, scholars, and the general public attempted to determine who—or what—was to blame for the disaster. In 1912, people in Great Britain and the United States placed great faith in the marvels of modern technology, which seemed to be lifting people out of an ignorant, inconvenient, and dangerous past. If the *Titanic* was infallible, then it was assumed that the officers and crew of the *Titanic* must have been responsible for sinking her. For many years the official and unofficial accounts of the disaster emphasized the risks taken by Captain Smith and the failure of the lookouts to spot the iceberg in time.

In more recent years, scientists and engineers have been taking a second look at the *Titanic* disaster—research that was spurred by the discovery of the wreck in twelve thousand feet of water in 1985. Although the damaged portion of the *Titanic* now lies beneath the sea bed, exploration of the buried hull by sonar, and a microscopic investigation of hull fragments brought to the surface, have led researchers to new conclusions. By one theory, the iceberg tore a series of long, thin slices along the joints between the ship's steel plates. The fracturing was made worse by the condition of the steel, turned brittle by the near-freezing water.

The sinking of the *Titanic* taught an important lesson concerning the actions and judgments of humans and the danger of presuming that any mortal creation can attain infallibility. As one breathless account in the *New York Sun* had it, "It is the old painful story of implicit faith in experience that proved valueless and in judgment that was fallible."[6] The lesson is one that the natural world teaches frequently, as it did more recently with the *Challenger* disaster, and as it does every time a train goes off the rails, an airline pilot misjudges a landing, or a computer falls prey to a virus. No matter how much money, ingenuity, and art is concentrated in any creation—whether a ship, a building, a bridge, a computer, or a rocket—it can still fall prey to the whims of the natural world, the weaknesses and machinations of human beings, and to the play of simple bad luck.

Notes

1. "Wreck of the Titanic," from the *Hampshire Chronicle*, April 20, 1912, www.hampshirechronicle.co.uk/titan.html.
2. From Lawrence Beesley, *The Loss of the S.S. Titanic: Its Story and Its Lessons*. Boston: Houghton-Mifflin, 1912. Quoted in David G. Brown, "The Last Log of the Titanic," from Encyclopedia Titanic, www.encyclopedia-titanica.org.
3. From speech of Senator William Alden Smith, May 28, 1912, on the Titanic Inquiry Project website, www.titanicinquiry.org/USInq/AmInq01.htm.
4. Stephen Cox, *The Titanic Story: Hard Choices, Dangerous Decisions*. Chicago and La Salle, IL: Open Court, 1999, p. 78.
5. The precise counts of victims and survivors of the *Titanic* disaster have eluded researchers and historians ever since the disaster. Even within some articles, the figures may vary widely.
6. From Marshall Everett, ed., *Wreck and Sinking of the Titanic: The Ocean's Greatest Disaster*. Chicago: Homewood Press, 1912, p. 98.

Chapter 1

Early Accounts and Inquiries

1

The *Hampshire Chronicle* Reports the Wreck of the *Titanic*

Hampshire Chronicle

The first news of the wreck of the *Titanic* reached New York via wireless messages sent by the Cunard liner *Carpathia*, the ship that rescued the *Titanic*'s survivors. In England and in the United States, panic struck the families of passengers and crew. Great crowds mobbed the offices of the *Titanic*'s owner and operator, White Star Line, a company that would not long survive the shipwreck and the bad publicity to follow.

The city of Southampton, the *Titanic*'s home port, suffered the worst. Here the *Titanic* had set sail on its maiden voyage on April 10, 1912, and here hundreds of the ship's crew members had their homes and families. On Saturday, April 20, the details of the disaster ran beneath banner headlines in the *Hampshire Chronicle*, Southampton's local newspaper.

WRECK OF THE *TITANIC*
APPALLING LOSS OF LIVES
WOMEN AND CHILDREN SAVED

A terrible disaster, unparalleled in the records of the sea, has overtaken the world's greatest ship, the White Star liner *Titanic*, which sailed from Southampton on Wednesday in last week on her maiden voyage to New York. Shortly after ten o'clock on Monday morning the news reached London that late on Sunday evening (United States time) the liner had been in collision in lat. 41.46 N., long. 50.14 W., with an

Reprinted from "Wreck of the Titanic," *Hampshire Chronicle*, April 20, 1912.

iceberg. At the moment of the disaster the vessel had made roughly two-thirds of her voyage to New York (3204 miles), and had just a thousand miles still to cover. Her nearest land point was Cape Race (Newfoundland), distant about 350 miles to starboard. On board the vessel were 2340 souls, comprising 350 first-class, 320 second-class, and 750 steerage passengers. The crew numbered 940. Early on Tuesday morning there came the terrible news that the *Titanic* had sunk within four hours of the collision, and a few minutes afterwards there was telegraphed the admission that many lives had been lost. The messages then to hand only accounted for the saving of 675 of the passengers and crew, "nearly all women and children."

Terrible Story Told by Cable

A Standard New York cablegram, dated New York, Tuesday, says:—

"The most appalling disaster in Mercantile Marine history has resulted, so far as can at present be ascertained, in the death of 1,252 souls and the rescue of 868. All the latter are on board the *Carpathia*, slowly making her way towards New York, through the same glacial sea of drifting ice which sent the *Titanic* to destruction.

"The *Virginia* and *Parisian* have announced definitely by wireless that they have no survivors on board, destroying the faint hope that the awful death list might be lessened.

"The *Titanic* drifted thirty-four miles after striking the iceberg and before she foundered.

"The Leyland liner *Californian* is continuing the search over a radius reaching out beyond this path for any possible raft or lifeboat still on the surface, but it is admitted that there is hardly a chance of the quest proving fruitful.

"A terrific thunderstorm which raged over Nova Scotia yesterday evening moved seaward in the direction of the *Titanic* disaster to-day, and would seem to have destroyed any chance that an improvised raft may be buoying up a few final survivors.

"The *Carpathia*'s wireless apparatus is sending slowly the names of survivors. Of 201 first cabin passengers thus far accounted for, 132 are women, 63 men and six children. Of 114 second-class, 88 are women, 16 men, and 10 children.

"The constant use of the wireless to send the names of the living prevents the transmission of any details of the catastrophe. All that is known is that Neptune thrust an icy hand beneath the waters, and crushed the mighty *Titanic* as if to scorn her name.

"How death came suddenly out of the chilling fog, how the frightened passengers gathered amid the useless luxury of the palatial liner, strapping lifebelts on one another; how the fearful cry, 'Women and children to the boats,' rang out as distress rockets tried to blaze a gleam of light through the overhanging pall; who were the heroes, who—if any—were the cowards when confronted with this swift ending of their human hopes; how the democracy of death made all men equal; how the Anglo-Saxon spirit sprang forth and lifted the lowliest immigrant woman in her weakness above the millionaire when the most crucial of all earthly tests came—these are things that the wireless has not yet had an opportunity to tell, and, may be, the world must wait until the *Carpathia*, with her pitiful consignment of widows and orphans, arrives to relate the story by word of mouth.

"She arrives in New York on Thursday evening or Friday morning, preferring to take the longer course to the southern haven rather than attempt to gain the nearer Canadian port, and risk an encounter with that northern ice which sent the *Titanic* to her grave.

"New York was stunned this morning when she awoke to the realisation that yesterday's wireless messages were all untrue, and that the real facts of the *Titanic's* fate had been suppressed. It is understood that the White Star officials first realised the awful extent of the disaster at two p.m. yesterday, but held back the news, hoping against hope, until late at night, when they were driven by the final passage of all doubt to announce the appalling death-roll.

"By the time the White Star offices opened in Lower Broadway this morning the front of the Shipping Trust's building was blocked with people, many weeping hysterically, inquiring for more news than was contained in the slow-arriving list of survivors. Police reserves were summoned, but had not the heart to drive away the pitiful, struggling crowds of relatives, who refused to disperse while a chance remained that the names they vainly looked for would appear in the next list received. Rich and poor mingled their grief as sober-faced clerks behind the counter gave negative answers to their passionate inquiries.

"The land wireless stations having lost touch with the

Carpathia, the Government has ordered the cruiser *Salem*, which is one of the most powerful wireless ships in the United States Navy, having a radius of a thousand miles, to proceed from Hampton Roads to convoy the *Carpathia* in and act as a relay ship for handling messages."

Very little could be added on Thursday to the reliable information already published regarding the disaster. What little news there was was bad. On Wednesday night the White Star Line in London received the following cable from their New York offices:—"The *Carpathia* is now in communication with Saisconset, and reports 705 survivors aboard." It is very difficult indeed to explain away the fact that this message points to a reduction of the previous official figure of 868 survivors. Throughout Wednesday the figure 705 persistently cropped up in New York advices, and although optimists still pinned their faith to the previous day's messages, and explained that 'survivors' perhaps did not include members of the crew, there was nevertheless a feeling that the death-roll might prove to be 163 heavier than even the terrible telegrams of Monday evening had indicated.

The Vessel Two Miles Down

The *Titanic* is lying, roughly, 12,000 feet deep, or considerably over two miles below the surface of the water. At that great depth the pressure of the water is about 2 and a half tons to the square inch. The conditions of pressure at this depth—as far below the surface as the average height of the Swiss Alps—are extraordinary. At 12,000 ft. deep a man would bear upon his body a weight equal to that of twenty locomotive engines, each with a long goods train loaded with pig iron. Under this enormous pressure the luxurious fittings of the gigantic liner are probably crushed like so much tissue paper, the water-tight doors of unflooded parts of the vessel smashed in and furniture possibly compressed out of shape. Strange tricks must have been played with the rich decorations and the elaborate effects of saloons and cabins. In the absolute stillness of the depths of the ocean, where there is perpetual night, the *Titanic* must remain. Any attempt at salvage is utterly out of the question. At depths of about 200 ft. divers suffer great hardships; at the depth at which the *Titanic* is resting diving is absolutely impossible. Only by some strange and mighty upheaval of Nature can the lost liner ever be exposed again to the gaze of human beings.

Scenes of Grief in London

Throughout the whole of Tuesday London lived in an atmosphere of suspense waiting for the wireless messages which came through the air with their words of comfort or desolation, or, almost worst still, bringing neither the one nor the other, but leaving a sharper pain of gnawing anxiety in the hearts of those whose near and dear ones were on the doomed vessel.

In the City offices and restaurants the one topic of conversation was the wreck and the latest cable. Every successive edition of the newspapers was eagerly bought up as soon as it appeared in the streets, and every hopeful rumour gave rise to a fresh burst of high optimism, each in its turn to be slowly but remorselessly worn away by succeeding reports.

On the buildings of all the shipping companies, and on many private business houses, the flags were flying at half-mast, and in the neighbourhood of the White Star Line's offices in Cockspur Street the crowds of people conversing in peculiarly hushed tones and the white drawn faces bore eloquent testimony to the tragedy which had occurred.

At the White Star Line's London offices in Oceanic House, over which the flags were flying at half-mast, the same scenes of anxious suspense were witnessed throughout the whole day.

Gloom in Southampton

In Southampton people to the last moment clung to the hope that better news of the *Titanic* would be received, but on Tuesday afternoon the whole town was overcome with gloom.

Flags were at half-mast on the public buildings and in the docks, and a meeting of the Harbour Board called for the afternoon was abandoned as a mark of sympathy with the sufferers. A letter was read from Colonel Philipps, M.P. for the borough, expressing his deepest sympathy with the inhabitants, and the Mayor said that the sympathy of Southampton and of all the civilized world went out to the sufferers from the frightful calamity. On his initiative a vote of condolence was adopted. One member of the Harbour Board had a son on board the *Titanic*, and an ex-member of the Board was a passenger.

Nearly a thousand families in Southampton are directly concerned in the fate of the crew alone, and in most cases the only breadwinner of the family has been lost. It is impossible to walk through the principal streets without meeting people who had friends on board, and the majority of the officers and crew were well known in the port. The shipping offices of the White Star Line were besieged all day by distressed women, for since the report was received that a considerable number of the crew had been saved there was keen anxiety for further particulars. In some of the poorer streets, where firemen and seafarers live in large numbers, very sad sights were witnessed. In some streets nearly every house was represented on board the *Titanic*, and the manner in which the bereaved women fastened on to the faintest glimmer of fresh intelligence was painfully pathetic.

It was reported on Wednesday night that many relatives with brief periods of intermission have been waiting continuously for 24 hours for tidings of the breadwinners of many humble homes. The suspense is agonising, and many heart-rending scenes have been witnessed.

The President of the Shipping Federation has telegraphed to the Mayor of Southampton that the Federation will give 2000 guineas to his relief fund for the distressed dependants of the crew of the *Titanic*.

Many agencies are at work in Southampton for the relief of the distress occasioned by the loss of so many of the *Titanic*'s crew. The Mayor on Wednesday paid a visit to the Lord Mayor of London, to confer with him as to the measures to be taken.

Sympathetic reference was made to the disaster before the business of the Borough Police Court was proceeded with on Tuesday morning. The Mayor (Councillor H. Bowyer, R.N.R.) said he felt sure he would be expressing the regret, which would be shared not only by the people of Southampton, but by the people in the whole world, at the awful calamity which had befallen the *Titanic*. As yet, they had had no definite information, but they hoped to hear later that the loss of life was not so great as they were led to believe. They knew the ship had gone, and it seemed incredible that out of the 3000 people on board everybody could have been saved. They feared there must have been some loss of life, but they hoped the loss of life was not so great as was feared. While the statement was being made, the Bench, and the officials, and the solicitors practising in Court, remained standing.

2
A Tragedy Caused by Misplaced Confidence

New York Sun

Soon after the *Titanic*'s sinking, the *New York Sun* editorialized that the ship had been traveling dangerously fast when it struck the fatal iceberg. In order to make good time, the ship's captain had failed to slow down while moving through the fields of ice or to change course to avoid the hazard. According to the *Sun*, this failure resulted not from criminal negligence but from the captain's underestimation of the danger and his excessive confidence that his ship was unsinkable.

This article was later reprinted in *Wreck and Sinking of the Titanic*, a 1912-era "instant book" that collected some of the best writing on the *Titanic* from a variety of sources.

The investigation of a committee of the United States Senate brought out all the material facts bearing upon the disaster that sent the *Titanic* and 1,595 persons to the bottom of the Atlantic. Mr. Bruce Ismay, managing director of the White Star Line, the first witness, deposed under oath that at the time of the collision the ship was not going at full speed. That is a matter of deduction from his testimony. "The ship's full speed was 78 revolutions. We did not make more than 72." The *Titanic* could steam between 22 and 23 knots an hour, so it is evident that her speed was at the rate of about 21 knots, and therefore high in an ice drift where bergs could be seen by daylight and might be encountered suddenly after dark.

It was a clear, starlit night, the sea was calm, and except

Excerpted from "The Responsibility for Fatal Speed," by *The New York Sun*, in *Wreck and Sinking of the Titanic*, edited by Marshall Everett. Chicago: Homewood Press, 1912.

for the presence of loose floes and masses of ice with submerged bases there was no reason why the *Titanic* should not have been making good time. But the exception was very important. Obviously the great ship was proceeding at a high rate of speed under orders of the captain, who just as obviously was trying to carry out the instructions of his employers. If the *Titanic* was not as fast a ship as the *Lusitania* or the *Mauretania* she was expected to make a good record on her maiden trip, which could not be done unless she held to a prescribed route. It was certainly in the power of Mr. Ismay to have the *Titanic*'s course changed to the south when dangerous ice was reported ahead. The warning had come by wireless from the *Amerika* the day before the disaster. But to take at once a more southerly course would have involved a loss in time of several hours at least on the maiden voyage of the great *Titanic*.

> *To the commander of the* Titanic, . . . *the conditions that destroyed his ship presented no perils requiring him to slow down to headway speed or to safe manoeuvering speed.*

After the tragic event it seems criminal that the course was not changed if the new ship was to be driven on at a speed of 21 knots. The alternative was to proceed slowly through the ice field, but at a rate to keep her under perfect control. A steamship of the size of the *Titanic* must maintain a speed proportionately greater than the speed at which a vessel of half her tonnage can be handled in an emergency. What, then, is the explanation of her forging through ice-strewn water almost at maximum velocity? Can there be any doubt that the risk was not understood? Swiftly to condemn is to lose sight of the fact that the experience of captains of transatlantic liners with fields of ice, particularly with bergs partly submerged, is negligible. To the commander of the *Titanic*, a veteran who had made the passage hundreds of times, the conditions that destroyed his ship presented no perils requiring him to slow down to headway speed or to safe manoeuvering speed. It was sufficient for him that the night was clear, that the ice was loose. He believed, as he had declared before he took charge of the ship, that she was unsinkable. A faith fatal in its consequences, but he knew nothing of the power of a great mass of floating ice to tear out the side of a 45,000-ton ship and smash in her watertight compartments. It is clear enough that the loss of the *Titanic* and the sacrifice of two-thirds of her passengers and crew was due more to ignorance and misplaced confidence than to criminal carelessness.

After the event the world knows that a fearful risk was taken that ought to have been avoided. It is the old painful story of implicit faith in experience that proved valueless and in judgment that was fallible. A thousand and a half lives seem to have been wantonly sacrificed, but to place the responsibility without mitigation is not as simple as it seems in the shadow of the awful disaster. The verdict will be pronounced unflinchingly, but let the investigation be deliberate and the evidence complete.—*New York Sun.*

3

The *Titanic*'s Crew Ineptly Handled the Ship's Lifeboats

Marshall Everett

The following selection was excerpted from *Wreck and Sinking of the Titanic*, a compilation of articles on the disaster published in 1912. In it, Marshall Everett reveals that the ship's crew had little experience in handling the ship's lifeboats and that lifeboat drills were not held as required. Thus, the crew was poorly prepared when disaster struck and failed to effectively deploy the lifeboats, resulting in the loss of many lives. Everett also reports a little-known fact: A coal fire was burning steadily from the day the *Titanic* left its home port.

There was some criticism among the survivors of the *Titanic* crew's inability to handle the lifeboats. "The crew of the *Titanic* was a new one, of course," declared Mrs. George N. Stone of Cincinnati, "and had never been through a lifeboat drill, or any training in the rudiments of launching, manning and equipping the boats. Scores of lives were thus ruthlessly wasted, a sacrifice to inefficiency. Had there been any sea running, instead of the glassy calm that prevailed, not a single passenger would have safely reached the surface of the water. The men did not know how to lower the boats; the boats were not provisioned; many of the sailors could not handle an oar with reasonable skill."

Albert Major, steward of the *Titanic*, admitted that there

Excerpted from "Other Contributing Causes of the Disaster," in *Wreck and Sinking of the Titanic*, edited by Marshall Everett. Chicago: Homewood Press, 1912.

had been no boat drills and that the lifeboats were poorly handled.

"One thing comes to my mind above all else as I live over again the sinking of the *Titanic*," he said. "We of the crew realized at the start of the trouble that we were unorganized, and, although every man did his best, we were hindered in getting the best results because we could not pull together.

"There had not been a single boat drill on the *Titanic*. The only time we were brought together was when we were mustered for roll call about 9 o'clock on the morning we sailed. From Wednesday noon until Sunday nearly five days passed, but there was no boat drill."

The White Star liner *Titanic* was on fire from the day she sailed from Southampton. Her officers and crew knew it, for they had fought the fire for days.

> *The White Star liner* Titanic *was on fire from the day she sailed from Southampton. Her officers and crew knew it, for they had fought the fire for days.*

This story, told for the first time on the day of landing by the survivors of the crew who were sent back to England on board the Red Star liner *Lapland*, was only one of the many thrilling tales of the first—and last—voyage of the *Titanic*.

"The *Titanic* sailed from Southampton on Wednesday, April 10, at noon," said J. Dilley, fireman on the *Titanic*, who lives at 21 Milton Road, Newington, London, North, and who sailed with 150 other members of the *Titanic*'s crew on the *Lapland*.

"I was assigned to the *Titanic* from the *Oceanic*, where I had served as a fireman. From the day we sailed the *Titanic* was on fire, and my sole duty, together with eleven other men, had been to fight that fire. We had made no headway against it.

"Of course, sir," he went on, "the passengers knew nothing of the fire. Do you think, sir, we'd have let them know about it? No, sir.

"The fire started in bunker No. 6. There were hundreds of tons of coal stored there. The coal on top of the bunker was wet, as all the coal should have been, but down at the bottom of the bunker the coal had been permitted to get dry.

"The dry coal at the bottom of the pile took fire, sir, and smoldered for days. The wet coal on top kept the flames from coming through, but down in the bottom of the bunker, sir, the flames was a-raging.

"Two men from each watch of stokers were told off, sir, to fight that fire. The stokers, you know, sir, work four hours at a time, so twelve of us was fighting flames from the day we put out of Southampton until we hit the iceberg.

"No, sir, we didn't get that fire out, and among the stokers there was talk, sir, that we'd have to empty the big coal bunkers after we'd put our passengers off in New York and then call on the fireboats there to help us put out the fire.

"But we didn't need such help. It was right under bunker No. 6 that the iceberg tore the biggest hole in the *Titanic*, and the flood of water that came through, sir, put out the fire that our tons and tons of water had not been able to get rid of.

"The stokers were beginning to get alarmed over it but the officers told us to keep our mouths shut—they didn't want to alarm the passengers."

Another story told by members of the *Titanic*'s crew was of a fire which is said to have started in one of the coal bunkers of the vessel shortly after she left her dock at Southampton, and which was not extinguished until Saturday afternoon. The story, as told by a fireman was as follows:

"It had been necessary to take the coal out of sections 2 and 3 on the starboard side, forward, and when the water came rushing in after the collision with the ice the bulkheads would not hold because they did not have the supporting weight of the coal. Somebody reported to Chief Engineer Bell that the forward bulkhead had given way and the engineer replied: 'My God, we are lost.'

"The engineers stayed by the pumps and went down with the ship. The firemen and stokers were sent on deck five minutes before the *Titanic* sank, when it was seen that they would inevitably be lost if they stayed longer at their work of trying to keep the fires in the boilers and the pumps at work. The lights burned to the last because the dynamos were run by oil engines."

4

Captain Smith's Indifference to Danger Contributed to the Tragedy

William Alden Smith

The *Titanic* disaster utterly consumed the public's attention for many days after the event. On Tuesday, April 16, the news prompted Senator William Alden Smith, who had once sailed with the *Titanic*'s Captain Edward J. Smith, to demand action of some kind—any kind—from President Taft, from the Justice Department, or from the U.S. Congress. The next morning, Senator Smith asked his Senate colleagues to pass a resolution authorizing a congressional investigation, to be held by the Committee on Commerce. The resolution passed, Senator Smith was appointed the subcommittee chairman, and an equal number of Republicans and Democrats were appointed to sit beside him. On the eighteenth, the Department of the Navy reported that certain messages of J. Bruce Ismay, the chairman of the White Star Line and a *Titanic* survivor, had been intercepted. To Senator Smith's alarm, the messages revealed that Ismay planned to return to England immediately with the crew. Senator Smith headed him off with subpoenas served dockside in New York harbor.

    The subcommittee met for eighteen days, heard eighty-six witnesses (beginning with Ismay), and generated a one-thousand-page transcript of questions, answers, evidence, and speeches. At the conclusion of the hearings, on May 28, 1912, Senator Smith rose in front of the Senate to harshly criticize the operation of the ship, the training of its crew, and the lack of sufficient lifeboats. But Senator Smith saved his most critical

Excerpted from a speech before the U.S. Senate, by William Alden Smith, May 28, 1912.

words for Captain Smith, claiming that the captain's indifference to the danger of passing ice caused the loss of the ship and of fifteen hundred lives.

IN THE SENATE OF THE UNITED STATES,
Tuesday, May 28, 1912.

Mr. President, my associates and myself return the commission handed to us on the 18th day of April last, directing an immediate inquiry into "the causes leading up to the destruction of the steamship *Titanic*, with its attendant and unparalleled loss of life, so shocking to the people of the world." Mindful of the responsibility of our office, we desire the Senate to know that in the execution of its command we have been guided solely by the public interest and a desire to meet the expectations of our associates without bias, prejudice, sensationalism, or slander of the living or dead. That duty, we believed, would be best performed by an exact ascertainment of the true state of affairs.

To the Judgment Seat

We went to the side of the hospital ship with purpose and pity and saw the almost lifeless survivors in their garments of woe—joy and sorrow so intermingled that it was difficult to discern light from shadow, and the sad scene was only varied by the cry of reunited loved ones whose mutual grief was written in the language of creation.

At 10 o'clock on that fateful Sunday evening this latest maritime creation was cutting its first pathway through the North Atlantic Ocean with scarcely a ripple to retard its progress.

From the builders' hands she was plunged straightway to her fate and christening salvos acclaimed at once her birth and death. Builders of renown had launched her on the billows with confident assurance of her strength, while every port rang with praise for their achievement; shipbuilding to them was both a science and a religion; parent ships and sister ships had easily withstood the waves, while the mark of their hammer was all that was needed to give assurance of the high quality of the work. In the construction of the *Titanic* no limit of cost circumscribed their endeavor, and when this vessel took its place at the head of the line

Indifference to Danger Contributed to the Tragedy 31

every modern improvement in shipbuilding was supposed to have been realized; so confident were they that both owner and builder were eager to go upon the trial trip; no sufficient tests were made of boilers or bulkheads or gearing or equipment, and no life-saving or signal devices were reviewed; officers and crew were strangers to one another and passengers to both; neither was familiar with the vessel or its implements or tools; no drill or station practice or helpful discipline disturbed the tranquility of that voyage, and when the crisis came a state of absolute unpreparedness stupefied both passengers and crew, and in their despair the ship went down, carrying as needless a sacrifice of noble women and brave men as ever clustered about the Judgment Seat in any single moment of passing time.

We shall leave to the honest judgment of England its painstaking chastisement of the British Board of Trade, to whose laxity of regulation and hasty inspection the world is largely indebted for this awful fatality. Of contributing causes there were very many. In the face of warning signals, speed was increased, and messages of danger seemed to stimulate her to action rather than to persuade her to fear.

At noon on that fatal Sunday the steamship *Baltic* warned her of ice within 5 miles of her track and near the place where the accident occurred; at 5 o'clock in the afternoon, and again an hour before the accident, when but a few miles away, the steamship *Californian* signaled the *Titanic* to beware of danger, which her operator curtly acknowledged; the same evening the *Titanic* transmitted to the Hydrographic Office in Washington a message from the steamship *Amerika*, saying she had passed "two large icebergs" near the track of the ill-fated ship. In the face of these warnings, each revolution of her engines marked at the moment of the collision her highest speed of 24½ miles per hour.

The *Titanic* rushed onward on her true course—one recognized as appropriate and agreed upon by mariners as the international highway for westbound vessels, yet dangerous at this season of the year, when the Labrador current may be bearing vast masses of ice across the track of ships. Scores of these towering glaciers planted themselves in the very pathway of this ship, and were so large and so numerous that, in the absence of fog, they should have been easily discernible by the lookout, who says in his testimony that if he had been supplied with glasses, such as he had been accustomed to on the *Oceanic*, and on this vessel, between Belfast and Southampton, but which were denied him by Second Officer Lightoller between Southampton and the place of this accident, he could have seen the iceberg with which this ship collided, "soon enough to get out of the way."

One of these icebergs was nearly 200 feet above the level of the sea, with seven-eighths of its ponderous bulk hidden beneath the surface. They are composed of ice and earth and rock, and old sailors of the coast of Newfoundland usually give them a wide berth. Land has been formed by these deposits, and icebergs have frequently grounded in 20 fathoms of water with protruding spires more than a hundred feet in height. As they go southward their journey is slow and erratic, and the influence of spring often causes explosions in the ice, which frequently serve to warn sailors of danger; sometimes the drift of field ice, led by a great berg, has been known to convoy schooners in a calm, while shipwrecked sailors have drifted hundreds of miles in safety upon the irregular surface of the ice. Skillful seamanship finds little difficulty in avoiding these obstacles, and those most familiar with the North Atlantic are usually alert at this season of the year to avoid unnecessary peril.

Captain Smith's Indifference to Danger

Capt. [Edward J.] Smith knew the sea and his clear eye and steady hand had often guided his ship through dangerous paths. For 40 years storms sought in vain to vex him or menace his craft. But once before in all his honorable career was his pride humbled or his vessel maimed. Each new advancing type of ship built by his company was handed over to him as a reward for faithful services and as an evidence of confidence in his skill. Strong of limb, intent of purpose, pure in character, dauntless as a sailor should be, he walked the deck of his majestic structure as master of her keel.

Titanic though she was, his indifference to danger was one of the direct and contributing causes of this unnecessary tragedy, while his own willingness to die was the expiating evidence of his fitness to live. Those of us who knew him well—not in anger, but in sorrow—file one specific charge against him: Overconfidence and neglect to heed the oft-repeated warnings of his friends. But in his horrible dismay, when his brain was afire with honest retribution, we can still see, in his manly bearing and his tender solicitude for the safety of women and little children, some traces of his lofty spirit when dark clouds lowered all about him and angry elements stripped him of his command. His devotion to his craft, even "as it writhed and twisted and struggled" for mastery over its foe, calmed the fears of many of the stricken multitude who hung upon his words, lending dignity to a parting scene as inspiring as it is beautiful to remember.

> *[Captain Smith's] indifference to danger was one of the direct and contributing causes of this unnecessary tragedy, while his own willingness to die was the expiating evidence of his fitness to live.*

The mastery of his indifference to danger, when other and less pretentious vessels doubled their lookout or stopped their engines, finds no reasonable hypothesis in conjecture or speculation; science in shipbuilding was supposed to have attained perfection and to have spoken her last word; mastery of the ocean had at last been achieved; but overconfidence seems to have dulled the faculties usually so alert. With the atmosphere literally charged with warning signals and wireless messages registering their last appeal, the stokers in the engine room fed their fires with fresh fuel, registering in that dangerous place her fastest speed.

President [managing director] Ismay testified:

> My recollection is that between Southampton and Cherbourg we ran at 60 revolutions, from Cherbourg to Queenstown at 70 revolutions, and when we left Queenstown we were running at 72 revolutions, and I believe that the ship was worked up to 75 revolutions, or about 22 knots per hour, but I really have no accurate knowledge of that.

And he again said, when asked if she was running at her maximum speed at the time she was making 75 revolutions:

> No, sir; my understanding is, or I am told, that the engines were balanced and would run their best at 78 revolutions.

It has been said many times—often in my hearing and often by letter—that the last dinner which he had partaken in the café of the ship, given by Mr. and Mrs. Widener, of Philadelphia, might have had some influence upon the action of the captain, but I have the word of the hostess, whose husband was lost in this catastrophe, that at that dinner Capt. Smith touched no liquor of any kind; indeed, that he asked that all glasses be removed from his plate. I make this statement because I think it is due to the memory of the dead, whose habits of life are worthy the highest praise.

The Water Rushes In

Last Saturday, in company with Admiral Watt, of the Navy, I visited the *Olympic*, a sister ship of the *Titanic*, just before she sailed from New York. Down deep in the bottom of that ship, 24 feet below the level of the sea, I found the head fireman of the *Titanic*, and there in the grease and the heat, by a dim light and surrounded by his companions, he swore that he was the first man to see the water come through the sides of the stricken ship. He said that the tear extended through the side of the forward fireroom, that the water came from a point about 20 feet below the sea level, and rushed like a mighty torrent into the ship.

We know from those who gave the order to construct the ship that the designer of the *Titanic* [Thomas Andrews] and *Olympic*, who was himself aboard the *Titanic* and did not survive, a young man but 39 years of age, designed the ship to carry safely two of her watertight compartments full of water in case of accident, the presumption being that by collision but one bulkhead and at most two of her watertight compartments would be injured, in which event, the watertight doors being closed, the ship could carry this additional weight without serious danger.

By the supplementary testimony of this head fireman, I am able to say that five compartments filled almost instantly. He also said that at the time the ship struck the iceberg the indicator in the fireroom displayed the letters "full speed," and that the ship had been running full speed during the entire afternoon and evening; that 24 of her boilers were lighted out of the 29, and at no other time on the voyage were so many boilers lighted; that when he received a bell signal he looked hastily to the indicator and found that the white light, "full speed," had been taken from the indicator and the red light, "stop," had been substituted in its place. Instantly the watertight doors between the firerooms were closed, but the danger had been accomplished, the harm had been done, and through a space extending past four bulkheads a tear had been made in that steel bottom admitting more water than the ship was able to carry. The water came in with tremendous force, and within five minutes after she struck the ship listed about 5 degrees.

I then reached a conclusion which, in my opinion, accounts for the small proportion of steerage who were saved. The occupants of the forward steerage were the first of the passengers to realize the danger. One or two witnesses said they stepped out of their berths into water probably an inch or two inches deep. Those in the forward steerage knew directly of the impact and of the presence of water, which came up from the lower part of the ship into the mail room and the forward steerage. Those steerage passengers went on deck and as fast as they were able took places in the lifeboats, while the after steerage, more than an eighth of a mile away, was by the operation of the added weight raised out of the water. That after steerage was a deck higher than the forward steerage, and was lifted higher and higher until the ship finally disappeared, so that these steerage passengers got their first warning of real danger as the angle of the deck became very great. I feel that the small number of steerage survivors was thus due to the fact that they got no definite warning before the ship was really doomed, when most of the lifeboats had departed. . . .

Senator Smith's Recommendations

The calamity through which we have just passed has left traces of sorrow everywhere; hearts have been broken and deep anguish unexpressed; art will typify with master hand its lavish contribution to the sea; soldiers of state and masters of trade will receive the homage which is their honest due; hills will be cleft in search of marble white enough to symbolize these heroic deeds, and, where kinship is the only tie that binds the lowly to the humble home bereft of son or mother or father, little groups of kinsfolk will recount, around the kitchen fire, the traits of human sympathy in those who went down with the ship. These are choice pictures in the treasure house of affections, but even these will sometime fade; the sea is the place permanently to honor our dead; this should be the occasion for a new birth of vigilance, and future generations must accord to this event a crowning motive for better things.

Recently we have witnessed a marked concentration of control of ocean transportation. Three companies—the International Mercantile Marine Co., the Hamburg-American Co., and the Royal Mail Steam Packet Co.—control 604 ocean steamers with a gross tonnage of 3,632,233 tons. These companies control more tonnage than the total American tonnage of all classes on the Great Lakes—2,943,523 tons. Any one of these companies controls tonnage nine times as great as the over-sea steam tonnage of the United States, and twice as great as the total registered steam tonnage of the merchant marine of the United States.

Regulation of steamship transportation is as necessary as regulation of railroad transportation, and less difficult to obtain. Transportation by rail is conducted through settled localities, where many residents would quickly discover and immediately report any irregularities or disregard of safety requirements, while by water it is conducted beyond the criticism of any except the actual passengers of the ship, making it all the more necessary for definite regulations.

Lanes of travel must be more carefully defined, strength of bow more positive, and [there must be] watertight subdivision to limit submergence, life-saving equipment better and numerous enough for all, discipline and practice a rudimentary exaction, eye more keen and ear alert to catch the warning cry. As on British battleships as well as on our own, powerful lights should be provided for merchant vessels to search out the partially submerged derelict; buoys should be carried by every ship to mark temporarily the place of the ship's burial in case of accident; and men of strength and spirit there must be, won back to a calling already demoralized and decadent. But 10 percent of the men before the mast in our merchant marine are natives or naturalized Americans; even England, that 20 years ago had barely 7,000 orientals on her merchant ships, now carries over 70,000 of that alien race. Americans must reenlist in this service, they must become the soldiers of the sea, and, whether on lookout, on deck, or at the wheel, whether able or common seamen, they should be better paid for their labor and more highly honored in their calling; their rights must be respected, and their work carefully performed;

harsh and severe restraining statutes must be repealed, and a new dignity given this important field of labor.

"In our imagination we can see again the proud ship instinct with life and energy, with active figures again swarming upon its decks"; musicians, teachers, artists, and authors; soldiers and sailors and men of large affairs; brave men and noble women of every land. We can see the unpretentious and the lowly, progenitors of the great and strong, turning their back upon the Old World, where endurance is to them no longer a virtue, and looking hopefully to the new. At the very moment of their greatest joy "the ship suddenly reels, mutilated and groaning." With splendid courage the musicians fill the last moments with sympathetic melody. "The ship wearily gives up the unequal battle. Only a vestige remains of the men and women that but a moment before quickened her spacious apartments with human hopes and passions, sorrows, and joys." Upon that broken hull new vows were taken, new fealty expressed, old love renewed, and those who had been devoted in friendship and companions in life went proudly and defiantly on the last life pilgrimage together. In such a heritage we must feel ourselves more intimately related to the sea than ever before, and henceforth it will send back to us on its rising tide the cheering salutations from those we have lost.

5

The *Titanic*'s Navigators Are Found Negligent

Geoffrey Marcus

The sinking of the Titanic brought tragedy to thousands of friends and relatives of lost passengers and crew. It also brought scathing press attacks, inquiries on both sides of the Atlantic, and lawsuits to the White Star Line. Yet while Captain Edward Smith and his officers, as well as Captain Stanley Lord of the *Californian*, came in for official blame, the inquiries absolved the White Star Line and the Leyland Line of any negligence or responsibility. It was concluded that no corporate officer could be blamed for hazardous ice conditions, overconfidence (aboard the *Titanic*), overcautiousness (aboard the *Californian*), and sheer bad luck.

An Irish farmer named Thomas Ryan was not completely satisfied, however. Ryan, who lost a son on the *Titanic*, sued the White Star Line and its corporate officers, charging liability and demanding damages. The case, which began in June 1913 in an English civil court, attracted little of the fanfare or publicity surrounding the official inquiries. As Geoffrey Marcus describes it in *The Maiden Voyage*, excerpted here, the new venue was ideal for a serious and evenhanded analysis of the actions of the *Titanic*'s officers and lookouts and the events of the sinking. In the end, the jury found the lookouts not guilty of inattention but its officers guilty of proceeding at an unsafe speed and violating the "duty of careful navigation."

The [British] Inquiry into the loss of the *Titanic* had lasted for thirty-six days, in the course of which ninety-

Excerpted from "Negligent Navigation," from *The Maiden Voyage*, by Geoffrey Marcus. Copyright © 1969 by Geoffrey Marcus. Reprinted by permission of Viking Penguin, a division of Penguin Putnam Inc.

eight witnesses had been examined and more than 25,600 questions asked; it was the longest and most detailed Inquiry ever held by a Wreck Court; and the general impression was that the last word had been said about the disaster.

'It is difficult to suppose, for instance,' commented the *Daily Telegraph* on July 31st, 'that any court which had to inquire into the question of the responsibility of the owners of the ship would disregard the expression of opinion of Lord Mersey and those who sat with him. The report having, in effect, acquitted them of all blame, it is not likely that any attempt will be made hereafter to establish the contrary.'

That was where the *Daily Telegraph* was wrong. Undaunted by the power and resources of the big battalions which would assuredly be ranged against him, a small farmer from County Cork, named Thomas Ryan, who had lost a son in the disaster, had the temerity to challenge this verdict, and presently took the matter to law. It was the first of several actions successively brought to recover damages for the death of persons who had lost their lives while passengers in the *Titanic*.

The Question of Negligence

The case of *Ryan v. Oceanic Steam Navigation Company* opened on June 20th, 1913, before Mr. Justice Bailhache and a Special jury. The plaintiff, Thomas Ryan, sued the defendants, the Oceanic Steam Navigation Company, otherwise the White Star Line, to recover damages for the death of his son, Patrick Ryan, who lost his life while in the defendants' vessel, the *Titanic*, owing to the negligence of the defendants' servants. Mr Campbell, K.C., and Mr Scanlan appeared for the plaintiff; and Mr Duke, K.C., and Mr Maurice Hill, K.C., and Mr Raeburn for the defendants.

Thus action was joined once more on the crucial issues of the disaster. The case was fought on much the same evidence, and with many of the same witnesses. But the atmosphere of the King's Bench was very different from that of the Scottish Hall: there was no model of the lost liner dominating the scene, no throng of fashionably attired spectators; there was none of the emotionalism, none of the almost theatrical touches which had characterized the Inquiry. The legal attitude to all these matters was calm, detached, shrewd, and analytical. As the arguments, examinations, and cross-examinations proceeded, the inherent weakness of the case for the owners and officers of the *Titanic* began to appear. The vulnerable points of the defendants' case came under strong and continuous attack: whereas at the Inquiry Lord Mersey, though obviously doubtful and uneasy, had not cared to probe too deeply. The professional reputation of poor 'E.J.' [Captain Edward J. Smith] was no longer regarded as sacrosanct, nor could his owners find safe shelter behind it.

> *As the arguments, examinations, and cross-examinations proceeded, the inherent weakness of the case for the owners and officers of the* Titanic *began to appear.*

Mr Campbell opened his case with the assertion that the question of negligence they had to consider was one of degree, and he could conceive no case in which the admitted facts more conclusively proved gross negligence than the present. They could have gone more south and avoided the ice, or slowed down. What happened? The enormous obstacle was not seen by any official on the ship until they were within five hundred yards of it. The vessel travelled that distance in thirty-seven seconds, and, having failed to take any precautions, nothing could then be done. They had not abated the full speed of the vessel through the danger zone, and although they saw the berg five hundred yards away they were unable owing to the speed of the ship to deflect it so as to pass safely by. Why was not the iceberg detected before? He believed it could be established that the berg could have been seen a mile away. Why was it not seen? There was no increase that night in the number of the lookout. It consisted of two men in the crow's nest and an officer on the bridge—the ordinary watch in perfect weather on a safe route. The grave omission was this. These icebergs looked on from a height were not easy to detect as if you were on a plane with them. There should have been a stemhead look-out, who would have seen the berg without having to look down on it from above. The look-out men had look-out glasses from Belfast to Southampton, but at Southampton they were taken from them. They would say that if they had had glasses they could have detected the ice much sooner than they did. . . . The defendants were in this dilemma. Assume their case was that the conditions were so unfavourable that they could not see a berg until it was quite close, what was their excuse for not reducing speed? If, on the other hand, the conditions were so favourable that they could see the berg easily, why did they not see it? The omission to do so was damning evidence of negligence.

A Lack of Ordinary Care

Mr Duke, in opening the case for the defendants, said that what was relied on here was not that Captain Smith and the other officers of the *Titanic* fell into some error of judgment, but that they were guilty of a lack of proper ordinary and reasonable care. That was an appalling proposition. Captain Smith was as fine and capable and high-minded a seaman as ever sailed the seas. The men who were involved had been the pick of the merchant service of this country. The *Titanic* was the finest product of modern shipbuilding.

It was said that the Captain had been warned of the presence of ice and had disregarded the warnings. Every warning had in fact been taken into account. That day and every day the rule was that such a notice should be fixed up in a conspicuous position for those concerned to see. That had been done. The survivors would tell the jury what had been done; how the course had been worked out and the probable position of the ice ascertained.

It was said that in these circumstances it was negligent to maintain this speed. Captain Smith and each one of the officers was responsible for the safety of this ship; yet it had not occurred to any one of them they were not doing the proper thing in keeping on this speed. Where were the seamen of any position or responsibility who said that it was a negligent thing to navigate the Atlantic in these circumstances at that speed? The jury would be told ... that in the presence of ice the safest course was to keep a sharp look-out and to go ahead at full speed and get out of the ice region.

Examined by Campbell, [wireless operator] Harold Bride declared that the duty of operators with regard to messages affecting the navigation of the ship was to take them to a responsible officer; that such telegrams had priority over private messages; that if he had received an important ice-report he would have passed it on immediately. He added, that was his practice and [Jack] Phillips's as well.

Stanley Herbert Adams of the *Mesaba* also gave evidence. He said that he had received no reply to the ice warning he had sent the *Titanic* from his Captain. It had been acknowledged by the operator on duty in the ship's wireless station; that was all. As to whether the telegrams had been taken up on the bridge or not, there was no conclusive evidence either way.

> *The jury would be told . . . that in the presence of ice the safest course was to keep a sharp lookout and to go ahead at full speed and get out of the ice region.*

Joseph Scarrott, A.B., said that he had been in the duty watch at the time of the collision. His duty was to 'stand by' for any orders that were given. Campbell asked him:

'Would a man at the stemhead have a better opportunity of look-out than a man in the crow's nest?'

'That would depend upon the atmosphere,' was Scarrott's reply. He said that he thought the iceberg could have been seen for about one thousand yards from the crow's nest.

'Would powerful glasses assist you?'

'I prefer glasses,' said the witness.

He testified that he had heard conversation among the crew that night to the effect that they were expecting ice.

Reginald Robinson Lee was examined by Mr Campbell with regard to the visibility at the time of the collision. He said that conditions that night were not favourable for a clear view. Part of the berg was above the haze. When he sighted the berg he did not think he could see the lower part of it below the haze. If the whole berg had been enveloped in haze he could not have seen it so soon.

'From the time you saw the berg,' Campbell asked, 'was it possible to avoid it?'

'Half a minute more,' replied Lee, 'would have been enough to avoid it.'

He said that the berg faced the ship with its dark side. He had seen a berg which presented its dark side when off St John's, Newfoundland. The reason he had not seen this berg before was because it presented its dark side; he thought he might have sighted it some minutes earlier if it had presented the ordinary white appearance of ice; it was higher than the foc'sle—it was as high as the boat deck. He said that he had not known the North Atlantic without a swell before this occasion. The sea was quite smooth. It was most unusual; it was an oily sea. The consequence was that there was no 'lipper of water' around the iceberg when it loomed ahead; if there had been it would have made breakers and they could have seen it. In the normal condition of the sea in the North Atlantic he would have sighted the iceberg earlier. Two or three hours after he left the ship, Lee added, a breeze sprang up.

Seeing the Haze

Lee's evidence was strongly controverted by [Charles] Lightoller, who once again spoke up in defence of the Western Ocean mail boat tradition of navigation. He said if he had seen the haze spoken of by the look-out man he would have reported it to the Master, and, if necessary, reduced the speed of the ship on his own initiative. He had reason to doubt the evidence given by the look-out men as to the existence of haze. He did not believe there was any haze. The reasons why the iceberg was not seen earlier were as follows. There was no moon. There was no ripple. The black side of the iceberg faced the ship. There was no swell. If the iceberg were seen five hundred yards away he did not think that the collision was inevitable. If the helm had been whipped over and one of the engines put astern, he said, the *Titanic* might possibly have cleared the berg.

However, Lightoller was obliged to admit that he could not remember whether he had actually passed on Captain Smith's order to [William] Murdoch about their having to slow down 'if it became in the slightest degree hazy.'

Cross-examined by Campbell, Frederick Fleet, the other look-out who had been in the crow's nest at the time of the collision, said he saw the haze for about a quarter of an hour before the impact. It was right ahead of him, he said, he could have picked up the object soon enough to have given notice in time to avoid the accident.

The evidence of Captain E.G. Cannons, of the Atlantic Transport Company, called as an expert witness on behalf of the defendants, was of special interest and importance. Cross-examined by Campbell, it appeared that Captain Cannons, in the same circumstances, would not, after all, have acted in the same way as Captain Smith. Captain Cannons declared that he had received as many as four messages a day regarding ice, but that it was an unusual occurrence. If all the five marconigrams [telegrams] mentioned in the case had been received by responsible officers, they would have indicated a particularly dangerous area. If he knew he was approaching such an area, he would take the precaution of slowing up, although he knew the night was clear. The *Masaba* report was more alarming than the first three. Assuming that he had received it, he would, if nothing were sighted, have navigated his vessel to the first longitude mentioned at full speed, having everybody on the alert, and would then have eased up. With his own ship, whose speed was 16 knots, if he saw a berg right ahead he could alter her course so as to avoid it in sixteen seconds.

Captain Cannons further testified that in the neighbourhood of an abundance of ice the atmosphere had a tendency to become hazy or foggy. He said that icebergs sometimes turned turtle and came up again. It was a sight which once seen was never forgotten. When the berg came up the ice was a bluish colour, but after exposure to the air it became white again.

The importance of Captain Cannons' evidence was, first, because of its implied criticism of the Western Ocean mail boat school of navigation; and, secondly, because it tended to corroborate the evidence of a number of witnesses who had testified to the existence of haze in the vicinity of 41° 46' N., 50° 14' W. on the night of the disaster. So far as the present case was concerned, it put a different complexion on affairs.

The other masters declared that they would have acted in the same way as Captain Smith. Captain Pritchard, formerly of the Cunard Line, when examined by Duke testified that he could stop the *Mauretania* running at 26 knots in three-quarters of a mile, and could alter course in ten seconds. Captain Hayes said that he had had long experience of the Atlantic crossing. In clear weather in the ice region it was his practice to maintain his course and full speed. He said that when he received reports of ice in clear weather his practice was to carry on the ordinary routine of the ship. The danger in the ice region was not a danger of ice, but a danger of fog. In clear weather a berg could be seen from five to six miles away at night. He said that he had been an officer under Captain Smith for five or six years, and that the latter was a careful navigator, who never took a risk, or in his opinion, came to an unwise decision. He also knew Mr Murdoch, who had been an officer under him, and said that he was a capable, efficient, and zealous officer.

The Dictates of Experience

In his closing speech, Duke fell back on the same line of defence, in its essentials, as had been successfully employed at the Inquiry. He maintained that the evidence which had been given showed conclusively that on a dark night an iceberg could be seen at a distance of four miles, and according to the rules of conduct on the sea employed by prudent seamen those in charge of the *Titanic* were justified, when the look-out was set, in proceeding on the assumption that a berg would be visible at that distance. The range of sight for ordinary eyes was four miles. The turning circle of the *Titanic* was 440 yards. Where was the imprudence, with a sufficient look-out and a ship perfectly under control, of going within four miles of an iceberg which you could avoid in two seconds? Here was a well-found ship capable of facing and meeting those perils of the sea which had to be looked for in the North Atlantic. Care was exercised in the setting of the look-out and in the observance of the course and speed of the vessel. He maintained attention had been given to the dictates of experience, and it was impossible that the jury should hold the defendants, by their servants, guilty of negligence or find that Captain Smith or Mr Murdoch had failed in their duty. That, in essence, was the counsel's defence against the charge of negligence.

In his reply, Campbell dealt with the question whether any haze on the night of the accident prevented the look-out men from having a clear view, and he submitted that there was a strong body of testimony that such was the case. Whether the *Mesaba*'s message was received or not, the messages admittedly received indicated that the ship was approaching a particularly dangerous area, in which it was necessary to exercise the greatest possible care. With regard to the nature of the iceberg with which the collision took place he would assume that it was as black as the defendants' witnesses had painted it. Even in that case Mr Lightoller said that it would be visible at some distance because there would be something white about it from whatever side it was approached. In view of such evidence, how could it be said that this disaster was due to the berg being black?

The counsel referred to the fact that the look-out men were not provided with glasses, and pointed out that it was significant that one of the men had said that if he had glasses in all probability he would have been able to see the berg in time to avoid the accident. The defendants were in a dilemma. If the accident were due to the iceberg being invisible by reason of a haze, then the defendants would be negligent in proceeding at full speed, because Captain Smith himself had said, 'If there is the slightest sign of haze we must go dead slow.' If, on the other hand, there was no haze and the look-out men could have seen the iceberg earlier and did not, then that would be negligence which would render the defendants liable.

In his summing up, Mr Justice Bailhache said that, with regard to the *Mesaba* message, if that had been received by a responsible officer it showed that there was ice right in front of the *Titanic*. If she ought to have slowed down on the receipt of the first three marconigrams, *a fortiori*, she ought to have done so on the *Mesaba* message. It was for the jury to consider whether that message had been received. In conclusion, the judge said that in substance nearly the whole case turned upon the question of the iceberg being black and not white, as was expected, and the jury must consider whether, in the face of the knowledge that there were occasional black bergs to be found which were difficult to see, and the fact that there was a discussion about them that night, it was negligent to run the *Titanic* at such a speed that if a black berg was met it could not be avoided. They must bear in mind that an experienced body of navigators of the highest class had said that in similar circumstances they would have acted in the same way as Captain Smith, while against that Captain Cannons had told them that if he had known there was ice in his course he would have slowed down.

The jury then retired; and after an absence of an hour and three-quarters they returned a verdict to the effect that the navigation of the *Titanic* was not negligent in regard to the look-out, but was so in respect of speed. They also found that there was not sufficient evidence to show whether the *Mesaba* message was communicated in due course to some responsible officer of the *Titanic*.

An Appeal and Judgment

Some time afterwards the Company took the case to the Court of Appeal; but it was dismissed on February 9th, 1914, Lord Justice Vaughan Williams delivering the following judgment.

The jury . . . returned a verdict to the effect that the navigation of the Titanic *was . . . [negligent] in respect of speed.*

'Was the ship negligently navigated in adopting the course which was adopted? There can be no doubt but that Captain Smith diverted his course and adopted the course which he did adopt by way of precaution to avoid the ice which he was warned against by marconigrams from the *Caronia* and *Baltic*, but it is said that, having regard to the terms of these messages, Captain Smith, having diverted his course to avoid the ice, had good reason to suppose that when after the diversion he approached nearer the "lane" the icebergs he was warned against had passed the "lane" in the direction of south or south-west. Against this it is said that the very diversion of the course of the ship in consequence of the marconigrams about the ice in the neighbourhood of the "lane" which constitutes the adopted course for this season of the year shows that Captain Smith at all events did not personally believe in the hard-and-fast application of the rule to maintain course and speed laid down by most of the expert witnesses. Moreover, the conversation between Captain Smith and Mr Lightoller showed that Lightoller had made calculations from which he inferred that it was likely that icebergs would be met about the time at which the collision in fact took place. This does not, to my mind, show that it was negligence to make the diversion which Captain Smith made, but it does show that he must have considered the question whether or not at the moment when he was returning to the "lane" he was not running into a dangerous region or zone. Now assuming that he had information that ought to have led him to the conclusion that he was running in such a dangerous region, Mr Lightoller was on duty at the moment of the conversation, and on the Captain's departing to his room actually ordered some precautions to be taken against collision with ice. So far as negligence is concerned, it makes no difference whether the negligence was the negligence of Lightoller or Captain Smith, or, indeed, the negligence of Murdoch, who succeeded Lightoller as the officer in charge shortly before the collision. . . . But the strength of the case against the ship rests on the knowledge or apprehension of danger which Lightoller certainly had, and Captain Smith possibly had. This inference which I draw is derived from the conversation between Captain Smith and Lightoller, and the orders given in apprehension of danger. The outcome of these considerations to my mind is that the only answer which the *Titanic* can give to the charge of negligent navigation in proceeding in the circumstances that I have narrated at full speed must be that it is the practice of ships navigated across the Atlantic by the most skilled navigators to maintain course and speed in such circumstances. But the evidence of Captain Cannons, an expert witness called on behalf of the plaintiffs, undoubtedly is capable of being understood as admitting that the circumstances may be of such a character as to require a departure by a prudent navigator from the general practice. Whether the occasion was such as to require a departure from the general practice was a question for the jury. The duty of careful navigation does not amount to a warranty against accidents causing damage in the course of the voyage; the duty of those navigating the ship is to use reasonable care. It is for the jury to find whether there has been a failure to perform this duty. If there is evidence upon which the jury may reasonably come to the conclusion that there has been such failure the verdict cannot be disturbed. To my mind it is impossible to say in the present case that there was no evidence upon which the jury might find, as they did, negligence. The diversion from the "lane" by the order of Captain Smith was itself clear evidence that he himself recognized the seriousness of the danger ahead of which he had notice, and was a recognition of the fact that even on a clear night you cannot always safely maintain course and speed in a region made dangerous by ice. The recognition of this is in fact the only excuse for the diversion from the course laid down by all the great shipping lines on November 15th, 1898.

'There is one other matter which I think is material, that is the defence that the condition of the sea and atmosphere and the failure to discover the proximity of the iceberg bring the case within the dictum of Mr Justice Bailhache in his summing up that "It is never negligence to fail to provide for the unforeseen or unforeseeable." I think that the danger in this case was neither unforeseen nor unforeseeable. There was warning, to my mind, of dangerous ice ahead, and the jury might reasonably come to the conclusion that in the circumstances a prudent master ought thereupon to have slowed down, or even to have stopped, and if the master failed to perform this duty he cannot say, "I am excused because the state of things which the ship afterwards encountered was unforeseen or unforeseeable"; as the accident might not have happened if he had slowed down.'

The judgment was from every point of view well and solidly grounded, distinguishing as it did the essential from the nonessential. It was based upon a far more accurate and dispassionate assessment of the evidence than had been the case at either the American or British Inquiry. The *ex parte* testimony given by Lightoller, which had hitherto carried so much weight, was heard yet again, considered, and finally discounted. 'E.J.'s' professional reputation was no longer unblemished. The charge of negligent navigation was upheld. *The danger was neither unforeseen nor unforeseeable.* That was the crux of the matter. The whitewash so liberally applied by Lord Mersey and his assessors had been effectively swept away and something like the true facts of the case exposed to view.

6

New Instructions for White Star Line Captains

White Star Line

The death of fifteen hundred passengers and crew members aboard the *Titanic*, the White Star Line's vaunted maritime showpiece, made the company suddenly safety-conscious. Shortly after the accident, and the British and American inquiries into it, the company issued new regulations to its captains, excerpted below, instructing them to place the safety of their ship and its passengers above all other concerns.

Captain _____

Liverpool.

Dear Sir,

In placing the steamer _____ temporarily under your command, we desire to direct your attention to the Company's regulations for the safe and efficient navigation of its vessels and also to impress upon you in the most forcible manner, the paramount and vital importance of exercising the utmost caution in the navigation of the ships and that the safety of the passengers and crew weighs with us *above and before* all other considerations.

You are to dismiss all idea of competitive passages with other vessels, and to concentrate your attention upon a cautious, prudent and ever watchful system of navigation which shall lose time or suffer any other temporary inconvenience

Reprinted from "Regulations Given to White Star Captains," by White Star Line, June 9, 1914. From "The Smoking Gun" website found at http://thesmokinggun.com/titanic/tregs.shtml.

rather than incur the slightest risk which can be avoided.

We request you to make an invariable practice of being yourself on deck and in full charge when the weather is thick or obscure, in all narrow waters and whenever the ship is within sixty miles of land, also that you will give a wide berth to all Headlands, Shoals and other positions involving peril, that where possible you will take cross bearings when approaching any coast. . . .

We have alluded, generally, to the subject of safe and watchful navigation, and we desire earnestly to impress on you how deeply these considerations affect not only the well-being, but the very existence of this company itself, and the injury which it would sustain in the event of any misfortune attending the management of your vessel, first from the blow which would be inflicted to the reputation of the Line, secondly from the pecuniary loss that would accrue (the Company being their own insurers), and thirdly from the interruption of a regular service upon which the success of the present organisation must necessarily depend.

We request your co-operation in achieving those satisfactory results which can only be obtained by unremitting care and prudence at all times, whether in the presence of danger or when by its absence you may be lured into a false sense of security; where there is least apparent peril the greatest danger often exists, a well-founded truism which cannot be too prominently borne in mind.

We are,
Yours truly

Chapter 2

The *Titanic* and the *Californian*

1

The Failures of the *Californian*'s Captain and Crew

C.V. Groves

The mystery of the *Californian* and the actions of its captain, Stanley Lord, have intrigued *Titanic* historians ever since the first confused wireless messages describing the disaster reached New York in the dawn hours of April 15, 1912. Sailing in the vicinity of the *Titanic*, the crew of the *Californian* had spotted a vessel about ten miles distant, apparently stationary, and firing white rockets. Rather than sail toward the mystery ship to investigate, Captain Lord kept the *Californian* right where she was. Ordering the deck officers to keep a watch on the ship, he then retired for the night, while his wireless operator also turned in after allowing the wireless set to run down. Early the next morning, the *Californian* finally received word of the disaster and steamed to the *Titanic*'s position—about four hours too late to rescue any survivors.

The actions of the *Californian* are debated to this day, with some answers provided by the many speculating *Titanic* experts and the eyewitness testimony of the *Californian*'s officers and crew. In 1957, a *Californian* officer, C.V. Groves, gave his side of the events in a third-person account entitled "The Middle Watch," offered in private to Walter Lord, the author of a popular account of the sinking entitled *A Night to Remember*. Groves's account went unpublished until 1998, when it was printed in the *Atlantic Daily Journal*, the official journal of the British *Titanic* Society.

Reprinted from "The Middle Watch," by C.V. Groves, 1957. From the "Titanic and Californian," website found at http://home.earthlink.net/~hiker1217/9Testimony/Midwatch.html. Reprinted with permission by The British Titanic Society.

The *Californian*, owned by the Leyland Line, was a four-masted steamship with a gross tonnage of 6,223 and a maximum speed of about 14 knots. She had accommodation for 50 passengers and carried a crew of 55 all told. Leaving London on Good Friday, April 5th, 1912, bound for Boston, USA, with a full cargo but no passengers, she was commanded by Captain Stanley Lord, a tall, lean man who had spent some 20 years at sea, much of which time had been in the North Atlantic trade. He was an austere type, utterly devoid of humour and even more reserved than is usual with those who occupy similar positions. Owing to a certain concatenation of circumstances he had obtained command somewhat earlier than was usual.

The Chief Officer was G.F. Stewart, a competent and experienced seaman nearing middle age who was well versed in the ways of the Western Ocean and was a certificated Master.

H. Stone, the Second Officer, had been some eight years at sea, the whole of which period had been spent in the North Atlantic and West Indian trades. He was a stolid, unimaginative type and possessed little self-confidence. He held a certificate as First Mate.

The Third Officer was C.V. Groves who had followed the sea as a career for six years and was in possession of a Second Mate's certificate. For three years his voyages had taken him mainly to South America and the Mediterranean. Latterly he had been engaged as a junior officer in the Indian and Colonial trades. Signalling was a strong point with him, for which he held the Board of Trade's special certificate, and he had made some progress as an amateur in wireless telegraphy.

The *Californian* carried one Apprentice and this was J. Gibson who had completed three years of his indentures with the Leyland Line, the whole of which time had been spent on the North Atlantic and West Indian runs. He was a bright lad, keen on his profession and one who showed every sign that he would make headway in it.

Ice Warnings

The voyage proceeded normally until the afternoon of Sunday April 14th, when, at a few minutes before 6.00 p.m., Mr. Groves went on to the bridge to relieve the Chief Officer for dinner. The sky was cloudless, the sea smooth and there was a light westerly breeze. Away to the southward and some five miles distant were three large flat-topped icebergs. Nothing else was in sight and the ship was making 11 knots through the water. Captain Lord was on the bridge talking to the Chief Officer as they scanned the horizon. A few minutes later they both went below for their meal, after which Mr. Stewart returned and relieved the Third Officer.

Mr. Groves went on watch again at eight o'clock to take over until midnight and was told by the Chief Officer that wireless messages had been received giving warning of ice ahead. Shortly afterwards, the Chief Officer went below. Almost immediately Captain Lord came up with similar information, telling him to keep a sharp lookout for this ice. The night was dark and brilliantly clear with not a breath of wind, and the sea showed no sign of movement, with the horizon only discernible by the fact that the stars could be seen disappearing below it. The lookout was doubled, there being a sailor on the forecastle head and another in the crow's nest. The Captain remained on the bridge with the ship proceeding at full speed, when suddenly the Third Officer perceived several white patches in the water ahead which he took to be a school of porpoises crossing the bows. Captain Lord evidently saw this at the same moment and as he was standing alongside the engine room telegraph he at once rang the engines full speed astern. In a very short space of time and before the ship had run her way off she was surrounded by light field ice. This was about 10.30 p.m. Despite the clarity of the atmosphere this ice was not sighted at a distance of more than 400 yards, nor was it seen by the lookouts before it was seen from the bridge.

Sighting the Stricken Ship

Captain Lord went below shortly after the ship had lost her way through the water, leaving instructions that he had to be called if anything was sighted. Absolute peace and quietness now prevailed save for brief snatches of "Annie Laurie" from an Irish voice which floated up through a stokehold ventilator. At 11.15 a light was observed three points abaft [to the stern side of] the starboard beam of which the Captain was immediately advised, and his reply to the information that it was a passenger ship was, 'That will be the *Titanic* on her maiden voyage.' This light was some 10 miles [distant] but he did not go up to look at it. Mr. Groves kept the ship under close observation and at 11.40 he saw her stop and then her deck lights were extinguished, or so it appeared to him. The time of the stopping of the ship is accurately fixed by the fact that at that moment the *Californian*'s bell was struck once in order to call the men who were to take over the middle watch. The dowsing of the lights caused no surprise to the Third Officer because for the preceding years he had sailed in large ships where it was customary to put the lights out at midnight to discourage the passengers from staying on deck too late.

> *Absolute peace and quietness now prevailed save for brief snatches of "Annie Laurie" from an Irish voice which floated up through a stokehold ventilator.*

Captain Lord was told of the ship having stopped and at a few minutes before the close of the watch he went up on the bridge and after looking at the distant ship observed 'That's not a passenger ship' to which the Third Officer replied 'It is, Sir,—when she stopped she put all her lights out.' The Captain then left the bridge saying that he must be told if that ship made a move, or if anything else hove into sight. The ship remained stationary. The drama had commenced.

At midnight Mr. Groves was relieved by Mr. Stone, to whom the Captain's orders were passed. The two young officers chatted for a while until the newcomer's eyes had got accustomed to the darkness. Mr. Groves then bade him 'Good night' and walked along the boat deck in order, as was his wont, to have a yarn with the sole Marconi Operator, Mr. Evans, before turning in. The Operator lay asleep in his bunk with a magazine in his hands. His visitor woke him up with the query 'What ships have you got, Sparks?' Dreamily he replied 'Only the *Titanic*.' He was then told she was in sight on the starboard beam. Almost mechanically the Third Officer picked up the wireless 'phones which lay on the operating table and placed them on his head to listen to what the ether might convey. He heard no sound, for he had failed to notice that the clockwork [batteries] of the magnetic detector had run down, thus no signals could be received until it had been wound up. He could read wireless signals when sent slowly. Mr. Evans had dropped off to sleep again and the 'phones were replaced on the table. The Third Officer closed the door and went to his room to turn in. The time was then 12.25 a.m. and that was ten minutes after the *Titanic* had commenced to send her messages of distress. The *Californian*'s operator slept peacefully on. The *Titanic* realised she was doomed and was lowering her lifeboats, and twelve hundred souls had seen their last sunrise.

About 6.45 that Monday morning the Third Officer was awakened by hearing ropes being thrown on to the boat deck above his head, and he realised that the boats were being prepared for swinging out.

Almost immediately Mr. Stewart came into his room to tell him to turn out as 'The *Titanic* has sunk and her passengers are in her boats ahead of us.' Jumping from his bunk Mr. Groves went across the alleyway to the Second Officer's room and asked if the news was true, and received the reply 'Yes, I saw her firing rockets in my watch.'

Arriving at the Scene

Amazed at hearing this, he went up on the bridge and found it to be a brilliantly fine morning with a light breeze and slight sea. There were more than 50 icebergs, large and small, in sight, and the ship was making slow way through the water. Some five miles distant a four masted steamship with one funnel was observed, and she proved to be the Cunarder *Carpathia*. She lay motionless with her house flag flying at half mast. The *Californian* arrived alongside her at about 7.30 and semaphore signals were exchanged from which it was learned that the *Titanic* had struck an iceberg at 11.40 the previous night and sunk two and a half hours later. Some 720 of her passengers had been rescued and the Carpathia was returning to New York forthwith. Would the *Californian* search the vicinity for further possible survivors? The Carpathia then got under way by which time it was nine o'clock, and less than 20 minutes later disappeared from view, hidden by the icebergs.

The sea was covered by a large number of deck chairs, planks and light wreckage. The *Californian* steamed close alongside all the lifeboats which the *Carpathia* had left floating, and it was particularly noted that they were empty. Scanning the sea with his binoculars, the Third Officer noticed a large icefloe a mile or so distant on which he saw figures moving, and drawing Captain Lord's attention to it, remarked that they might be human beings. He was told that they were seals. The *Californian* now made one complete turn to starboard followed by one to port and then resumed her passage to Boston passing the Canadian Pacific steamship *Mount Temple*, and another steamship of unknown nationality.

> *Scanning the sea with his binoculars, the Third Officer noticed a large icefloe a mile or so distant on which he saw figures moving, and drawing Captain Lord's attention to it, remarked that they might be human beings. He was told that they were seals.*

Before noon the *Californian* had cleared all the ice, and among many wireless messages she intercepted was one addressed to Mr. W.T. Stead, a passenger who was with those lost in the Titanic, offering him a dollar a word for his story of the casualty. It was sent by a well known New York newspaper.

The New England coast was approached in a dense fog out of which loomed a tugboat containing a number of American newspaper men expecting to obtain a story. Their journey was a vain one.

What was the complete story of events aboard the *Californian* during the middle watch of that fateful morning of April 15th? The passage of time has not dulled the recollections of all who were in any way concerned.

Mr. Stone and the Apprentice Gibson saw the ship which Mr. Groves had reported as being a passenger ship fire eight rockets, the first of which was seen at 1.10 a.m. This is the number which the *Titanic* is believed to have sent up between 1.00 and 2.00 a.m. and at 2.20 a.m. Mr. Stone reported to Captain Lord that the distant ship had 'disappeared.' It is known that the *Titanic* foundered at that time.

Officers of the *Titanic* and many others aboard her reported having seen the lights of a ship which was stopped a few miles away from her, and the passengers on the ill-fated vessel were reassured on being told by the officers that this ship would soon come to their assistance.

The Failures of the Californian's Captain and Crew

All that middle watch the *Californian* remained stationary, for news of the rockets being seen did not stir her Captain into action. Mr. Stone lacked the necessary initiative to insist upon his coming to the bridge to investigate things for himself, and it did not occur to him to call the Chief Officer when he realised the apathy of the Captain, who apparently slept peacefully whilst this drama was being enacted.

Mr. Stewart relieved the bridge at 4.00 a.m., when the events of the watch were related to him. Half an hour later he roused Captain Lord and when told about the rockets which had been fired, he replied to the effect that he knew all about them. Shortly before 6.00 a.m. Mr. Stewart was instructed to call the wireless operator to see if any information could be obtained regarding the distress signals, when advice was received from several ships of the sinking of the *Titanic*. Slowly at first but eventually at full speed, the *Californian* got under way until she arrived at the scene of the disaster.

Unanswered Questions Concerning the *Californian*

Many questions will forever remain unanswered concerning the failure of the *Californian* to render assistance to the stricken ship. Mr. Stone knew without a shadow of a doubt that there was trouble aboard the vessel from which the distress signals had been fired, but he failed to convince his Captain. But did Captain Lord need any convincing? Was Mr. Stone afraid that if he was too insistent he would arouse the wrath of his superior?

Why did Captain Lord take no efficient steps to render assistance before 6 o'clock? Did he consider problematical damage to his ship was of more importance than the saving of lives?

Many times the question of Captain Lord's sobriety on that occasion has been raised, but it cannot be too strongly asserted that he was a most temperate man and that alcohol played no part in the matter.

Does an experienced shipmaster lay down fully-clothed and in such circumstances sleep so heavily as he said he did on that night? Surely, surely, that is open to the very gravest of doubts.

Probably it would not be far from the mark if it is stated that the fate of those twelve hundred lost souls hinged on the fact that Mr. Groves failed to notice that the magnetic detector was not functioning when he placed the 'phones on his head in the wireless office at which time the ether was being rent by calls of distress which he would not have failed to recognise. And what of those figures on the icefloe? Were they only seals, as the Captain asserted? It has already been stated that all the *Titanic*'s lifeboats which were left afloat were closely examined and found to contain no occupants. A month later in almost the same spot the White Star liner the *Majestic* picked up one of these boats, and in it were found the bodies of passengers who had evidently died of starvation, for the ship's doctor who examined them reported the men's mouths contained fragments of cork from the lifebelts. Had these passengers escaped from the sea on to the icefloe and then eventually got into the boat as it drifted past?

> *It cannot be too strongly asserted that [Captain Lord] was a most temperate man and that alcohol played no part in the matter.*

What is the probable explanation of the *Titanic*'s deck lights appearing to go out when it is beyond dispute that they burned right up to the moment when she sank? She was approaching the *Californian* obliquely, and when she stopped she put her helm hard over and thus foreshortened her perspective thereby giving the appearance of the extinction of her lights.

The whole unfortunate occurrence was a combination of circumstances the like of which may never again be seen, and a middle watch which will not soon be forgotten.

2

The Captain of the *Californian* Defends Himself

Stanley Lord

Captain Stanley Lord of the *Californian* had a lot of explaining to do in the wake of the *Titanic* disaster. On the night of the tragedy, the crew of the *Californian* saw a ship nearby sending off rockets. Most commentators agree that this ship was the *Titanic* in distress, although Lord adamantly denied this.

After the sinking, Lord was brought before a British court of inquiry and thoroughly questioned. He had a plausible explanation for his inaction that night: The other ship had apparently steamed out of sight, and although his wireless operator had tried to raise her, he had been unsuccessful (as it later came out, because his wireless batteries had run down). His bosses at the Leyland Line could not fully accept the explanation, however, and Lord lost his post. Writers and movie directors would cast him as the villain in the *Titanic* tragedy, and Lord would spend the rest of his life defending his actions.

The following affidavit, written by Captain Lord in June 1959, neatly sums up Lord's own view of the affair. Lord expresses his sense of being wronged and misunderstood. At the end of the affidavit, he points out yet one more cruel irony of the *Titanic* disaster: the slander of his name and reputation at the hands of a namesake, the writer Walter Lord, whose own fame and reputation rested on a sensationalistic and, in Captain Lord's view, inaccurate account of the disaster.

Reprinted from "Affidavit of Captain Stanley Lord," from Appendix A of *The Titanic and the Californian*, edited by Peter Padfield. Copyright © 1965 by Peter Padfield.

I went to sea in 1891 as a cadet in the barque *Naiad* owned by Mr. J.B. Walmsley. After obtaining my Second Mate's Certificate of competency I served as Second Officer in the barque *Lurlei*. In February, 1901, I passed for Master and three months later obtained my Extra Master's Certificate.

I had entered the service of the West India and Pacific Steam Navigation Company in 1897. This company was bought by the Leyland Line in 1900 and I continued in their service, being appointed to command in 1906 at the age of twenty-nine.

In April, 1912, I was in command of the liner *Californian*, having sailed from London for Boston, U.S.A. on April 5th. On April 13th, noon latitude by observation was 43° 43' North; on 14th April, the noon position by observation was 42° 05'N, 47° 25'W, and course was altered to North 61° West (magnetic) to make due West (true). I steered this course to make longitude 51° West in latitude 42° North on account of ice reports which had been received.

At 5 p.m. on April 14th, two observations of the sun taken by the Second Officer, Mr H. Stone, to check the longitude were reported to me. These gave a run of 60 miles since noon, which was much ahead of dead reckoning. Another observation which I caused to be taken at 5.30 p.m. gave 64 miles since noon.

At 6.30 p.m. we passed three large icebergs 5 miles south of the ship. These I caused to be reported at 7.30 p.m. by wireless to the S.S. *Antillian*, the message being as follows: "*6.30 p.m. apparent ship's time, latitude 42° 5'N, longitude 49° 9'W, three bergs five miles southwards of us regards Lord.*" A little later I was informed that a routine exchange of signals with the *Titanic* showed that she had also received the message sent to the *Antillian*. These would appear to have been the same icebergs sighted and reported by wireless during the day by the *Parisian* in position 41° 55'N, 49° 14'W.

At 7.30 p.m. the Chief Officer, Mr G.F. Stewart, reported to me a latitude by Pole Star of 42° 5½'N. This with the previous observation for longitude gave me proof that the current was setting to WNW at about 1 knot.

At 8 p.m. I doubled the lookouts, there being a man in the crow's-nest and another on the fo'c'sle head.

At 8.5 p.m. I took charge on the bridge myself, the

Third Officer, Mr C.V. Groves, also being on duty. The weather was calm, clear and starry.

At 10.15 p.m. I observed a brightening along the western horizon. After watching this carefully for a few minutes I concluded that it was caused by ice. At 10.21 I personally rang the engine-room telegraph to full speed astern and ordered the helm hard aport. As these orders came into effect the lookout men reported ice ahead. Under the influence of the helm and propeller going astern the ship swung round to ENE by compass (NE true).

The ship was then stopped surrounded by loose ice and from one-quarter to half a mile from the edge of a low ice field. As I could not see any clear place to go through I decided to remain stopped until daylight. Allowing S 89° W (true) 120 miles from my noon position, and also taking into account the latitude by Pole Star at 7.30 p.m., I calculated my position as being 42° 5'N, 50° 7'W.

A Light to the East

At 10.30 p.m. as I was leaving the bridge, I pointed out to the Third Officer what I thought was a light to the eastward which he said he thought was a star.

I went down to the saloon deck and sent for the Chief Engineer. I notified him that I intended to remain stopped until daylight but he was to keep main steam handy in case we commenced to bump against the ice.

I pointed out to him the steamer I had previously seen approaching from the eastward and southward of us and about 10.55 p.m. we went to the wireless room. We met the wireless operator coming out and pointing out the other vessel to him I asked him what ships he had. He replied: "Only the *Titanic*." I thereupon remarked, judging from what I could see of the approaching vessel, which appeared to be a vessel of no great size and comparable with our own: "That isn't the *Titanic*." I told him to notify the *Titanic* that we were stopped and surrounded by ice in the position I had calculated, and he left at once to do so.

Later I noticed the green (starboard) light of the approaching vessel, also a few deck lights in addition to the one masthead light previously seen.

At 11.30 p.m. I noticed that the other steamer was stopped about 5 miles off, also that the Third Officer was morsing him. I continued watching and noticed that she didn't reply.

At 11.45 p.m. I went on to the bridge, casually noticed the other vessel, and commented to the Third Officer that she had stopped and wouldn't reply to our morse signals. He answered in the affirmative.

At ten minutes after midnight, it now being April 15th, the Second Officer came on to the saloon deck. I drew his attention to the fact that we were stopped and surrounded by ice and that I intended to remain stopped until daylight. I pointed out the other steamer to him, told him that she was stopped and that he was to watch her and let me know if we drifted any closer to her. He then went on to the bridge to relieve the Third Officer, and I went into the chartroom.

I sat there reading and smoking until 0.400 a.m. when I whistled up to the bridge through the speaking tube and asked the Second Officer if the other ship was any nearer. He replied that she was just the same and I told him to let me know if he wanted anything as I was going to lie down on the chartroom settee. I then did so, being fully dressed with boots on, etc., and with the electric light on. I left the watch on deck to the Second Officer with every confidence, as he was the holder of a British Board of Trade First Mate's Certificate of competency (foreign going) and my standing orders, which were well known to every officer, stated categorically that I was to be called at once in all cases of doubt.

"Something About a Rocket"

At about 1.15 a.m. the Second Officer whistled down to say that the other steamer was altering her bearing to the southwest and had fired a white rocket. I asked him whether it was a company's signal and he replied that he didn't know. I thereupon instructed him to call her up, find out what ship she was, and send the apprentice, James Gibson, down to report to me.

I then lay down again in the chartroom, being somewhat relieved in my mind at the news that the other ship was under way and removing herself from her earlier relatively close proximity. For some time I heard the clicking of the morse key, and after concluding that the Second Officer had succeeded in communicating with the other ship, I fell asleep.

Between 1.30 a.m. and 4.30 a.m. I have a recollection of Gibson opening the chartroom door and closing it immediately. I said: "What is it?" but he did not reply.

At 4.30 a.m. the Chief Officer called me and reported that it was breaking day and that the steamer which had

The Captain of the Californian *Defends Himself* 65

fired the rocket was still to the southward. I replied: "Yes, the Second Mate said something about a rocket."

I then went on to the bridge and was for some little time undecided as to the advisability of pushing through the ice or turning round to look for a clearer passage to the southeast. However, as daylight came in I could see clear water to the West of the icefield so put the engines on stand-by at about 5.15 a.m.

About this time the Chief Officer remarked that the steamer bearing SSE from us was a four-master with a yellow funnel and asked me whether I intended going to have a look at her. When I asked him why, he replied that she might have lost her rudder. I said: "She hasn't any signals up, has she?" He replied that she had not, but that the Second Officer had said that she had fired several rockets during his watch. I told him to call the wireless operator and see what ship it was. He did so but fifteen or twenty minutes later came back and reported that the *Titanic* had struck an iceberg and was sinking. Some delay was then experienced before we received an authoritative message giving the estimated position of the disaster but about 6 a.m. the following signal from the *Virginian* was handed to me: "Titanic *struck berg wants assistance urgent ship sinking passengers in boats his position lat 41° 46', long 50° 14', Gambell, Commander."*

Dawn Breaks on the *Californian*

This position I calculated to be about S16W, 19½ miles from our own estimated position. I immediately got under way and proceeded as quickly as possible on course between S and SW, pushing through about 2 to 3 miles of field ice. A lookout man was pulled in a basket to the main truck, given a pair of binoculars and instructed to look out for the *Titanic*.

At 6.30 a.m. I cleared the field ice and proceeded at full speed (70 revolutions). At 7.30 a.m. approximately, we passed the *Mount Temple* stopped in the reported position of the disaster. As there was no sign of any wreckage I proceeded further South, shortly afterwards passing a ship having a pink funnel and two masts, bound North, which turned out to be the *Almerian*.

A little later, I sighted a four-masted steamer to the SSE of us on the East side of the icefield, and received a verbal message from the wireless operator that the *Carpathia* was at the scene of the disaster. I steered to the South until the steamer was nearly abeam when I altered course and proceeded through the icefield at full speed, making for the other steamer. She proved to be *Carpathia* and I stopped alongside her at about 8.30 a.m. Messages were exchanged regarding the disaster and subsequent rescue operations.

At about 9.10 a.m. the *Carpathia* set course for New York and I continued the search for survivors, the ship steaming at full speed with the Second Officer and a lookout man in the crow's-nest. While carrying out this search, I saw the smoke of several steamers on the horizon in different directions. We passed about six wooden lifeboats afloat, one capsized in the wreckage; with the exception of two small trunks in a collapsible boat, the others appeared to be empty. At about 11.20 a.m. I abandoned the search and proceeded due West (true) through the ice, clearing same about 11.50 a.m. The *Mount Temple* was then in sight a considerable distance to the South West of us and heading to the westward.

The noon position was 41° 33'N, 50° 09'W; the latitude was taken under the most favourable conditions by the three officers and reported to me. I did not personally take an observation this day. From this observation I placed the wreckage in position 41° 33'N, 50° 01'W, being about SSE, 33 miles, from the position in which the *Californian* had stopped at 10.21 p.m. the previous evening.

The Second Officer stated that the rockets he saw did not appear to be distress rockets.

I later called for written reports on the events of the night from the Second Officer and Apprentice. In amplifying his report, the Second Officer stated that the rockets he saw did not appear to be distress rockets, as they did not go any higher than the other steamer's masthead light nor were any detonations heard which would have been the case under the prevailing conditions had explosive distress signals been fired by a ship so close at hand. In addition, the ship altered her bearings from SSE at 0.500 a.m. to SW½W at 2.10 a.m.; assuming her to have been 5 miles from the *Californian* when she stopped at 11.30 p.m., the distance she must have steamed to alter her bearing by this amount I calculate to have been at least 8 miles.

While on passage to Boston, wireless messages about the disaster were received from Captain Rostron of the *Carpathia*; the American newspapers *New York American, Boston Globe, Boston American* and *Boston Post*; a passenger in the *Olympic* called Wick; and the Leyland Line.

After our arrival at Boston at 4 a.m. on April 19th, I was summoned with the Radio Officer to appear before the United States Congressional Inquiry in Washington. I gave my evidence there in accordance with the above facts. Subsequently, I never had an opportunity to read a transcript of the proceedings or findings of this Inquiry, nor was the matter referred to by those I met on subsequent visits to American ports.

Return to England

After the return of the *Californian* to Liverpool, I reported to the Wreck Commissioner and to the Marine Superintendent of the Leyland Line, Captain Fry. While in the latter's office, Mr Groves, the Third Officer, volunteered the opinion that the ship seen from the *Californian* on the night of April 14th was the *Titanic*. This was the first occasion I had heard him make such a statement and I duly commented to this effect to the Marine Superintendent.

I was summoned by telegram to appear before the British Court of Inquiry in London on May 14th and travelled down from Liverpool the previous evening. When I arrived in Court, Mr Roberts, manager of the Leyland Line, introduced me to Mr Dunlop and told me he was watching the proceedings on behalf of the owners and officers of the *Californian*. Apart from the questions asked by Mr Dunlop when I was in the witness-box, I had no further conversation with him nor at any time was I afforded an opportunity to discuss the proceedings with him or to suggest what navigational and other technical facts might be brought out which would verify the truth of the evidence which I had given.

Captain Lord's Argument

Had I at any time been clearly warned—as I consider I should have been—that adverse findings in respect of the *Californian* were envisaged, I would have taken all possible steps during the Inquiry to call evidence to prove beyond doubt:

(a) *That the* Californian *was completely stopped*, with full electric navigation and deck lights burning, from 10.21 p.m. to 6 a.m. Additional evidence to prove this conclusively could have been provided by the production of the engine-room log-books covering that period and by the testimony of the Chief Engineer and those engineer officers who kept watch during the night.

If the Court could have been satisfied that the *Californian* was indeed stopped all night, then inevitably they would have had to conclude:

(i) that the *Californian* must have been beyond visual range of the actual position of the disaster, for in perfect visibility no other ship's lights were seen by the two lookout men and the two officers of the watch on the *Titanic* either before or immediately after she struck the iceberg, nor was the *Californian* in sight of the survivors as day broke. Additionally, none of the green flares burnt in the *Titanic*'s boats which were seen at extreme range from the *Carpathia* were seen from the *Californian*.

(ii) that the *Californian* could not have been the ship later sighted from the *Titanic* which led to the firing of rockets, for this ship was clearly seen to be under way; to approach from a hull-down position to turn; and to recede.

(b) *That from the navigational evidence the* Californian *must have been at least 25 miles from the position of the disaster.* Additional proof could have been supplied from the engine-room log-books to show how far she steamed from the time of getting under way at 6 a.m. to reaching the wreckage at 8.30; in addition, further detailed consideration should have been given to the relative movements, positions and astronomical observations of the *Californian, Carpathia, Mount Temple* and *Almerian* from before noon on the 14th to the evening of the 15th April in an endeavour to fix as accurately as possible the *actual* as distinct from the *estimated* position in which the wreckage and survivors were found. A further point to which the Court gave no consideration was the fact that the area in which the *Californian* lay stopped all night was covered with field ice extending as far as the eye could see; the area in which the *Carpathia* found the *Titanic*'s lifeboats contained very many large icebergs.

If the Court could have been satisfied that during the night the *Californian* was indeed at least 25 miles from the scene of the disaster, they would have had to conclude that even if the distant rocket signals beyond the near-by ship which were apparently seen from the *Californian* had been correctly identified as distress signals, and news of the disaster confirmed by wireless at the earliest possible moment, it would still have been quite impossible for us to have rendered any useful service, for bearing in mind the time taken to reach the wreckage in daylight, under the most favourable conditions, we could not have reached the survivors before the *Carpathia* did.

The Californian *could not have been the ship later sighted from the* Titanic *which led to the firing of rockets.*

Finally, I would have submitted for the Court's consideration the following two important points:

(*a*) That had I or the Third Officer any reason to conclude that the ship seen approaching from 10.30 p.m. onwards was a passenger ship steaming towards an icefield at 21 knots, then instinctively as practical seamen either one of us would have taken immediate action to warn her that she was standing into danger.

(*b*) That it was perfectly reasonable for the Second Officer to decide that no emergency action was called for when a ship which had been so close to the *Californian* as to cause concern, and which had completely failed to respond to persistent attempts to call her up by morse light, got under way and passed out of sight after substantially altering her bearing. This positive action was more than sufficient to nullify any previous concern which might have been created by her apparently making use of confusing rocket signals of low power reaching only to mast height, and lacking any explosive content or detonation such as was customarily associated with a distress rocket and which should have been perfectly audible in the calm conditions then obtaining.

I was also in Court on May 15th. I clearly recall that when Lord Mersey, the President [of the Inquiry], pressed Mr Groves, the Third Officer, to express his opinion that the ship seen from the *Californian* was the *Titanic*, Lord Mersey commented that this was also his opinion—a comment which does not appear in the official record of proceedings.

I returned to Liverpool on the evening of May 15th, being due to sail in the *Californian* on 18th. However, after my return home I was verbally informed by the Marine Superintendent that I was to be relieved and I accordingly removed my gear from the ship.

Letters and New Evidence

I first read the findings of the Court of Inquiry in the Press and while naturally not at all pleased at the references to myself, I was not unduly concerned as I was confident that matters would soon be put right. I immediately approached the Mercantile Marine Service Association, of which I was a member, and a letter putting my side of the case was published in the September, 1912, issue of the Association's magazine, *The Reporter*.

At a later stage, Mr A.M. Foweraker, of Carbis Bay, a gentleman whom I never met, but who took a great interest in my case, supplied a series of detailed analyses of the evidence which were published in *The Reporter* and also in the Nautical Magazine under the title of *A Miscarriage of Justice* (April, May and June issues).

Letters were addressed to the Board of Trade both by the M.M.S.A. and by myself requesting a rehearing of that part of the Inquiry relating to the *Californian*. This request was consistently refused. The M.M.S.A. also sent a letter to the Attorney-General (Sir Rufus Isaacs) requesting an explanation of the comment in his closing address that *"perhaps it would not be wise to speculate on the reason which prevented the Captain of the* Californian *from coming out of the chartroom"* on receiving the Second Officer's message at 11.15. This obvious reflection on my sobriety I greatly resented, for it was my invariable practice to refrain from taking alcohol in any form while at sea, quite apart from the fact that no previous reference to such a possibility had been made during the course of the Inquiry. The only reply received was that Sir Rufus was on holiday and must not be troubled with correspondence.

I received a letter dated August 6th, 1912, from a Mr Baker, who had served in the *Mount Temple* on her return voyage from Quebec. This appeared to indicate that she was the ship seen to approach and recede from the *Titanic*. Although this letter was brought to the attention of the Board of Trade, no action was taken.... Through Mr Baker, I met

The Captain of the Californian Defends Himself 71

Mr Notley, the officer referred to in Mr Baker's letters who had been taken out of the *Mount Temple*. He confirmed that he would give his evidence if called upon to do so, but could not volunteer information because of the adverse effect this might have upon his future employment—a conclusion with which I quite agreed.

I also corresponded with others whose evidence and opinion might prove of assistance to me and received letters from Captain Rostron of the *Carpathia*; Mr C.H. Lightoller (Second Officer of the *Titanic*); and Captain C.A. Bartlett, Marine Superintendent of the White Star Line.

Initially, I had been assured by the Liverpool Management of the Leyland Line that I would be reappointed to the *Californian*. However, I was later told privately by Mr Gordon, Private Secretary to Mr Roper (Head of the Liverpool office of the Leyland Line), that one of the London directors, a Mr Matheson, K.C., had threatened to resign if I were permitted to remain in the company, and on August 13th I was told by the Marine Superintendent that the company could not give me another ship. I then saw Mr Roper, who said that it was most unfortunate but the matter was out of his hands and public opinion was against me. I was therefore compelled to resign, up to which time I had been retained on full sea pay and bonus.

I continued my endeavours to obtain what I considered to be the justice due to me but without success, although I personally visited the House of Commons on October 23rd, 1912, and engaged in correspondence with the Board of Trade during 1913.

A New Posting

Toward the end of 1912, I was approached by Mr (later Sir) John Latta of Nitrate Producers Steam Ship Co. Ltd. (Lawther, Latta & Co.), who had apparently been approached on my behalf by a Mr Frank Strachan, United States agent for the Leyland Line, who had throughout done everything possible to assist me. After a visit to London to meet Mr Latta, I was offered an immediate command with the company and entered their service in February, 1913. I served at sea throughout the First World War, and as the aftermath of the *Titanic* Inquiry in those days was not such as to affect me personally or professionally in any way, I decided to let the matter drop.

I continued to serve in Lawther Latta's until ill-health compelled me to retire in March, 1927. Sir John Latta's opinion of my service as a shipmaster is given in the reference I received from the Company.

After my retirement, I was unaware of any adverse reference to the *Californian* in respect of the *Titanic* disaster, as I have never been a filmgoer and was not attracted towards any books on the subject. Latterly, my eyesight also began to deteriorate and the amount of reading I could do was consequently considerably curtailed. However, I noted some extracts from a book called *A Night to Remember* in the Liverpool evening newspaper, the *Liverpool Echo*, although the brief extracts which I read—which did not contain any reference to the *Californian*—did not impress me.

In the early summer of 1958, however, I became aware that a film also called *A Night to Remember* apparently gave great prominence to the allegation that the *Californian* stood by in close proximity to the sinking *Titanic*. I therefore personally called on Mr W.L.S. Harrison, General Secretary of the Mercantile Marine Service Association, of which organisation I had remained a member without a break from 1897.

Acting on my behalf, Mr Harrison entered into correspondence with the producers of the film, the publishers of the book and later the author, asking for them to give consideration to my side of the story. However, those concerned maintained that the British Inquiry findings were authoritative and provided sufficient justification for the references to the *Californian* in their publications.

Being desirous of avoiding undue publicity, which owing to my present age and failing health would undoubtedly have serious effects, I am making this sworn statement as a final truthful and authoritative record of what occurred when I was in command of the *Californian* on the night of April 14th, 1912.

SWORN by the above-named deponent Stanley Lord at 13 Kirkway, Wallasey, in the County of Chester, on this twenty-fifth day of June, 1959, before me, Herbert M. Allen, Notary Public.

(Signed) STANLEY LORD.

3

The Captain of the *Californian* May Have Acted Reasonably

Stephen Cox

In the following excerpt from his book *The Titanic Story: Hard Choices, Dangerous Decisions*, author Stephen Cox examines the actions of the *Titanic*'s first officer and the *Californian*'s captain on the night the *Titanic* sank. He concludes that both of these officers evaluated the risks of their respective situations and made reasonable decisions to act as they did. First Officer William Murdoch could have kept the *Titanic* from sinking by allowing the ship to hit the iceberg head-on; however, the tenets of good seamanship dictated that such a course of action was unthinkable.

Similarly, according to Cox, Captain Stanley Lord of the *Californian* may have acted wisely in choosing not to investigate the rockets seen by his crew, presumably set off by the sinking *Titanic*. It could be argued that the risks of attempting a nighttime rescue in treacherous, ice-filled waters justified his decision not to act.

Juggling with risks can have strange effects on moral judgment. Risks can be juggled away as if they had no weight at all; or they can become the focus of attention, until all that people can see is the heavy objects that keep landing in both their hands.

The first of those two effects appeared in the American public's response to [White Star Line Chairman] Bruce Ismay's moral problem. Before the *Titanic* disaster, it was uni-

Excerpted from *The Titanic Story: Hard Choices, Dangerous Decisions*, by Stephen Cox. Copyright © 1999 by Stephen Cox. Reprinted by permission of Open Court Publishing Company.

versally agreed that the managers of a steamship company had no business interfering with the management of the ships themselves. The risk was too high. (Given Ismay's ignorance of navigation, it was stupendously high.) There would also, quite obviously, be heavy risks involved if a corporate official tried to assume responsibility for the evacuation of a ship. Such a person could easily do more harm than good.

As it happened, Ismay assumed none of these risks. When he was handed the iceberg warning on April 14, he did not advise Captain [Edward J.] Smith to slow down. When the *Titanic* was sinking, Ismay helped other people enter the lifeboats, but he felt no duty to manage the operation or to go down with the ship as a consequence of his management responsibility. He acted like an ordinary passenger and entered a lifeboat when he saw no other passengers competing for the space. But popular opinion noticed only the fact that Ismay failed to make the *Titanic* slow down and failed to make sure that his fellow-passengers escaped. It took no account of the risks that he (and everyone else) would have run if he had tried to take charge.

Lord Mersey and his investigators [of the British inquiry] experienced the second effect of a juggling with risks. They never lost sight of the risks inherent in any decision, including the risk of pronouncing moral judgment. Sometimes, they were simply mesmerized by the risks appearing on either hand. They were particularly impressed by the strange case of the *Titanic*'s swerve.

Good Seamanship Destroyed the *Titanic*

When the lookouts told First Officer [William] Murdoch that there was an iceberg right ahead, Murdoch turned the ship to port; and *Titanic* nearly missed the iceberg. She did miss the violence of a head-on collision. But testimony showed that if Murdoch had decided to hit the berg head-on, *Titanic* would have repeated the famous experience of the *Arizona*: her bow would have crumpled, but her bulkheads would have held.* She would not have received the fatal wounds to her starboard side. She would have remained afloat. Even Ismay knew that. The 200 people who were

---

* In 1878, the passenger liner *Arizona* struck an iceberg head-on, but remained afloat.

sleeping closest to the bow would have died; but that would have been many fewer people than the 1,500 who did die.

One could easily conclude that the ideal officer would have calculated the risk of trying to swerve and the risk of not trying to swerve (the iceberg is close, the ship is heavy, the force of any collision will be tremendous), and would have decided to hold his course. No one, however, would have hailed such a person as the savior of 1,500 innocent people. Instead, everyone would have damned him as the murderer of 200 innocent people.

Still, [Lord Mersey] reflected, if Murdoch had held his course "he would have saved the ship."

This problem tormented Mersey and his assistants. They did not know what to do with it. Attorney General Isaacs tried going at it head-on. He said that if a liner were purposely driven into the ice, "I hope I am not on it, that is all." White Star's counsel Robert Finlay was determined to have things both ways, and in the strongest terms. He argued that "it would have been outrageously bad seamanship" for Murdoch *not* to have swerved, even though, "as things turned out," what he did "was unfortunate—most unfortunate." Mersey conceded that Murdoch exercised "good seamanship." Still, he reflected, if Murdoch had held his course he "would have saved the ship." Like White Star's lawyer, Mersey was juggling madly; but he was by no means happy with his act. Finally even he surrendered:

> It is not worth while discussing it. Have we got anything to do with it? We are all agreed that Murdoch was quite right in doing what he did.

That was that. Yet Mersey was not just trying to escape. He was being very careful. He had been thinking about the relationship between risk and moral responsibility. He was aware that his own inquiry could change that relationship. A running of risks that was quite innocent *before* the disaster might now, with improved awareness of one set of possible consequences, transform itself into [what the commissioner during "Final Arguments" characterized as] "negligence of a very gross kind."

That is what Mersey thought about Captain Smith's way of dealing with the risks of ice and speed. Of this, Mersey would write:

> I am not able to blame Captain Smith. He had not the experience which his own misfortune has afforded to those whom he has left behind, and he was doing only that which other skilled men would have done in the same position.

Still

> What was a mistake in the case of the "Titanic" would without doubt be negligence in any similar case in the future.

But Mersey was not prepared to tell seamen that they should take the risk of running their vessels into icebergs. Who knows what the result of such advice would be? Perhaps it would be some misfortune about which later investigators would write an instructive story. Mersey let that alone; *he* was too careful to run such risks. And yet, as he said, "a man may make, as we all know, a mistake which is due sometimes even to too great care." The risks remained heavy on both his hands.

Captain Lord's Decision

But how should one regard the too great care exercised by Captain Stanley Lord, master of the steamship *Californian* and provider of yet another strange episode in the *Titanic* story? Here was risk management—prudent, sober, perhaps even conscientious—but neither Mersey nor any of the other investigators was of two minds about it.

The *Californian* was a vessel of the Leyland line. It was owned, ironically, by the same [J.P.] Morgan holding company that owned White Star. On April 14, the *Californian* encountered field ice and stopped for the night. Another ship appeared in the vicinity and started firing rockets. Lord received reports about them, but he neglected to awaken his wireless operator to find out whether anything was wrong. Lord was sleepy, too; and he was concerned about the light ice that was bumping against his ship. The *Californian* sat still until morning. Then Lord had one of his officers wake up the wireless operator, who immediately discovered that the *Titanic* had foundered. Lord got the *Californian* going and maneuvered through the ice until he arrived, several hours too late, at the site of *Titanic*'s wreck. He kept all mention of rockets out of his log, and he hoped that no one would be the wiser.

> *[Captain Lord] kept all mention of rockets out of his log, and he hoped that no one would be the wiser.*

Regrettably for Captain Lord, stories from two of his crewmen got into the American press, and he was left to explain himself, somehow. He suggested that the *Titanic* was not visible from the *Californian*. It might have been *some other ship* that was firing rockets—which, as he preferred to think, were some shipping company's communications signals. These suggestions made people wonder why Captain Lord had not done his best to find out what was going on with that *other* ship. Some may also have wondered why the rockets of the other ship, coming as they did from the general direction of the *Titanic*, were not noticed on the *Titanic* herself, where anxious observers would have welcomed any sign of life in the surrounding ocean.

The real explanation, as Attorney General Isaacs surmised, was that Captain Lord, meeting field ice for the first time in his career, had decided that he did not want to test his own ship against the unaccustomed risk. It is possible that Lord was hesitant to rouse his wireless operator because he did not want to confirm the fact that another vessel was in distress and find himself obligated to do something about it. He weighed the risks, both from ice and from moral responsibility, and he tried to reduce them to the lowest possible level.

For this he was censured by Lord Mersey and Senator [William Alden] Smith, and he was fired by the Leyland line, which discovered that his inordinate skill at risk management had made him a distinct liability to public relations. Six months after his firing, he was offered a job by the Nitrate Producers Steamship Company, for which he would eventually command a ship larger than the *Californian*. He retired in 1928, when he was only 50 years old, and spent many comfortable years reading good books. In 1958, he happened to see the notice of a movie, *A Night to Remember*, that implied criticism of his actions in regard to the *Titanic*. He then appealed for vindication to the secretary of his professional group, the Mercantile Marine Service Association, who took up his cause. Since that time, people interested in the *Titanic* have hotly debated the nature of the decisions that Lord made, or evaded, on the night of her distress. An influential party of researchers is convinced, as Lord obviously convinced himself, that when the facts are viewed dispassionately they will demonstrate that his judgment was correct by normal standards of seamanship.

But suppose they won't. Suppose we accept the conventional view that Lord simply neglected to intervene in a situation that might have posed a danger to his ship. Lurking near that hypothesis is yet another glittering fact that can suddenly reverse itself and become a hazardous black berg. Why is it, one may ask, that Captain Lord of the *Californian* was blamed for his moral irresponsibility, while Captain [Arthur] Rostron of the *Carpathia* was honored, for his moral heroism, with a gold medal from Congress, the command of the great liners *Mauretania* and *Berengaria*, and the applause of the whole world?

The reply, of course, is that Rostron fulfilled the sailor's traditional notion of duty. [Second Officer Charles] Lightoller stated it in this way: "Absolutely no effort shall be spared in an endeavor to save life at sea. A man must even be prepared to hazard his ship and his life." But it might be argued that Lord also had a responsibility, the responsibility not to risk his ship and the lives of his crew unnecessarily. So he didn't. But Rostron took that risk, and more: Lord's ship carried no passengers; Rostron's carried almost 800. Would Rostron have become the hero of April 15, 1912, if he had driven the *Carpathia* at full speed onto one of the icebergs that littered her path? *Should* Rostron have become a hero for assuming such a serious risk, while Lord was denounced for refusing it? Perhaps public opinion was wrong again.

Chapter 3

Modern Perspectives on the Sinking of the *Titanic*

1
The *Titanic*'s Reckless Captain

Michael Davie

After the *Titanic* sinking, the public on both sides of the Atlantic felt a powerful, morbid curiosity: a mixture of horror, fascination, and a strong desire to know more. Much of the curiosity focused on the enigmatic Captain E.J. Smith, who had gone down with his ship. Who was the man behind the stolid, reassuring image, behind the grandfatherly beard and the fine blue uniform? For one thing, he was a man whose ability and decades of experience had earned him the most prestigious post at sea.

After the disaster, many writers took Captain Smith as the key player in the drama. Many portrayed him as an experienced old salt who simply placed too much faith in the marvels of modern engineering. In the following excerpt from his book *Titanic: The Death and Life of a Legend*, author Michael Davie also suggests that Captain Smith, for all of his ability and experience, suffered the fatal faults of recklessness and arrogance.

The *Titanic* sailed from Southampton on April 10 shortly after noon, bound for Cherbourg to pick up more passengers. Captain Smith must have known that the latest leviathans required careful handling. Six months earlier, when he was taking the *Olympic* out of Southampton on her sixth Atlantic crossing, she had collided with a cruiser, *HMS Hawke*, whose bow had torn a jagged and ugly gash ten feet deep in the *Olympic*'s starboard quarter. An Admiralty Court held that the *Olympic* had gone too close to the cruiser and

Excerpted from *Titanic: The Death and Life of a Legend*, by Michael Davie. Copyright © 1986 by Michael Davie. Reprinted by permission of Alfred A. Knopf, a division of Random House, Inc.

that White Star, and hence Captain Smith, were to blame for the collision. Smith had not been pleased; he wrote to a friend to say that "we are not taking it lying down." He meant that White Star would appeal, which it did; but the verdict was upheld. It was thought at the time that the huge bulk of the *Olympic* might have drawn the cruiser toward her. Two of Smith's officers on the *Titanic*, [Charles] Lightoller and William Murdoch, who was on watch when the *Titanic* hit the iceberg, were also aboard the *Olympic* when she hit the *Hawke*.

Smith must have been reminded of the *Hawke* when he stood on the bridge of his latest command as she in her turn left Southampton. A local paper described what happened. "The departure of the *Titanic* on her maiden voyage on Wednesday was marred by an untoward incident, which caused considerable consternation among the hundreds of people who had gathered at the quayside to witness the sailing of the largest vessel afloat," said the *Southampton Times & Hampshire Express*. The wash of the *Titanic* caused all six ropes holding the liner *New York* alongside the jetty to part. The greatest consternation was among the sightseers who had trespassed onto the *New York* to get a better view, for they thought a collision "inevitable." A touch ahead on the port engine by Captain Smith and the rapid intervention of two tugs saved the day. But it had been very close. The *Southampton Times* interviewed Captain C. Gale of the tug *Vulcan*. "We got hold of the *New York* when she was within four feet of the *Titanic*," he said. The paper ended its report by remarking that the trespassers aboard the *New York* "will doubtless retain for years vivid recollections of the first sailing of the *Titanic* from Southampton docks." The episode showed, for the second time, that lessons still had to be learned about the giant ships' maneuverability.

Was Captain Smith, behind the obscuring beard, a risk taker?

Was Captain Smith, behind the obscuring beard, a risk taker? Of all the characters in the *Titanic* drama, he seems now particularly hard to understand. Here was a ship's captain of vast experience, universally regarded as a highly responsible man, who behaved at times in a manner that appears, in retrospect, positively reckless. In his reminiscences, Lightoller recalls with approval the dash with which Smith used to take his ships into New York—"at full speed," says Lightoller, although the word "full" must be an exaggeration. "One particularly bad corner, known as the South-West Spit, used to make us fairly flush with pride as he swung her round, judging the distances to a nicety; she heeling over to the helm with only a few feet to spare between each end of the ship and the banks." According to Lightoller, Smith as a mailboat captain was relentless in the way he pressed on despite heavy seas and fog to get the mail through on time; this was one of the reasons why Lightoller admired and respected him. Robust captaincy was a function of intense competition between rival companies. But Cunard historians maintain that the White Star Line, which Cunard eventually took over, followed a particularly bold policy.

Did Captain Smith choose a daring route across the Atlantic for the *Titanic*? Well-connected elderly Englishmen recall well-connected friends saying years ago that the secret of the *Titanic* disaster was that she was taking a shortened route, too far north, because she was lacking coal as a result of the great 1912 coal strike. True, the strike gravely embarrassed the transatlantic-liner business. The *Olympic*, in New York on one crossing, crammed every available part of the ship with coal in order to boost White Star's reserves. The *Titanic* had to get coal in Southampton from other ships, which were consequently delayed. But the route she followed was normal. There were, and indeed still are, two recommended transatlantic tracks, the northern and the southern, which are alternated according to the time of year. *Titanic* was on the southern, not the northern, route. Immediately after the disaster, the recommended southern route was moved further south, and then further south again, to avoid any risk of a second collision. But though the *Titanic*'s route turned out to be fatal, there was nothing unusual about it.

Trying to understand Captain Smith's state of mind before the disaster, one is tempted to take his own word for it, as expressed to *The New York Times* [during a 1907 interview], and conclude that his errors stemmed from a belief that the dangers of the Atlantic had been neutralized by technology—that modern transatlantic travel had become safe and predictable. But there was too much daily evidence to the contrary for Captain Smith to have really believed anything of the sort. Newspapers reported shipping accidents then as faithfully as they report airline accidents or alarms today. The files of *The New York Times* in the months before the sinking are full of such reports. On the first day of the new year the White Star liner *Arabic* arrived in New York a day late because of a gale. During the next few weeks, three crewmen of an American ship were swept overboard during a storm off Key West, Florida; the U.S. Atlantic Fleet lost two seamen when all of its ships were struck, and some of them badly damaged, by an Atlantic gale; a British battleship at Portsmouth broke its moorings in a storm and crashed into a dreadnought; fifty-three out of a crew of fifty-seven were drowned when a British steamer sank off Aberdeenshire during a gale; the White Star liner *Adriatic* arrived in New York thirty hours late because of high seas; the British steamer *Birchfield* arrived in New York having had a seven-day fire in its coal bunkers; the *Lusitania* was a day late because of bad weather and ice.

Dangers of Ice

No doubt Captain Smith, after a lifetime at sea, regarded these incidents as regular, familiar hazards of seagoing. Can he have thought the same about icebergs and failed to take them seriously? If not, why on the fourth day of the maiden voyage did he take his ship at high speed into a region he knew to contain icebergs?

There does seem to have been general underestimation of the fact, fully accepted now, that icebergs are the most dangerous hazard of all, more dangerous than storms, collisions, or fog. It is a pity that a long short story published in 1898 was not more widely read; it was written by a retired merchant navy officer and described how a ship called *Titan* collided with a huge iceberg. The correspondence with the *Titanic* disaster is so close that it was only when I had a first edition of the book in my hand that I could believe it was written before and not after 1912. The story was called "Futility" and the parallels are as follows:

	Titan (1898)	*Titanic* (1912)
Flag of registry	British	British
Time of sailing	April	April
Displacement (not gross) tons	70,000	60,000
Length	800 feet	882 feet
Propellers	Triple screw	Triple screw
Top speed	24–25 knots	24–25 knots
Capacity	About 3,000	About 3,000
Number aboard	2,000	About 2,227
Number of lifeboats	24	20
Capacity of lifeboats	500	1,178
Watertight bulkheads	19	15
Engines	3 triple expansion	2 triple expansion and one steam turbine
Side of ship struck	Starboard hull pierced by spur of iceberg	Starboard hull pierced by spur of iceberg

Only after the *Titanic* went down was the story noticed and alleged to have a special significance as an example of second sight.

Unlike the *Titan*, the *Titanic* before she hit the iceberg had received by wireless telegraph no fewer than six ice warnings. Decades later, a member of the *Titanic* Historical Society read a newspaper item that led to a visit to the small German industrial town of Leisnig in Saxony, where an old gentleman suddenly fumbled in his desk, produced a crumpled scrap of paper, and exclaimed, "If only they had heeded my warning!" The man's name was Otto Reuter; in April 1912 he had been first wireless officer aboard the German liner *Amerika*; and a scrawl on the piece of paper was the text of the radio telegram he sent via the Cape Race station to the U.S. Hydrographic Office in Washington at 11:20 a.m. on Sunday, April 14, the day the *Titanic* hit the iceberg. It read: "*Amerika* passed two large icebergs in 41 degrees 27 minutes N. 50 degrees 8 minutes W. on the 14th April Knuth." Knuth was the captain. The message was intercepted by the *Titanic* and passed on to Washington.

But Herr Reuter was only one of the message senders. On Friday the 12th the French liner *Touraine* told the *Titanic* she had crossed a "thick ice field." Besides the *Amerika*, on the fatal Sunday, the *Caronia* sent a message reporting "bergs, growlers and field ice"; the *Noordam*, after congratulating Smith on his new command, reported "much ice"; and the *Baltic* soon after midday passed on a report from a Greek steamer which said she had passed "icebergs and large quantities of field ice." How many of these wireless messages did Captain Smith see? One point to remember about wireless telegraphy in 1912 is that although not brand new, it was relatively new and not properly organized to meet a ship's needs. Wireless operators aboard the liners were employed not by the shipping company but, if they used the Marconi system, by the Marconi Company. No iron routine had yet been drilled into the operators about the treatment of wireless messages, although they were under instructions to give priority to any messages about navigation; still more inefficient, Marconi operators thought of themselves in competition with other wireless companies and often either declined to accept signals or treated them in a cavalier fashion. Smith certainly saw four messages. It came out in the inquiries that around lunchtime on Sunday the 14th he handed the *Baltic*'s message to Bruce Ismay, the White Star chairman traveling on the ship's maiden voyage, who put it in his pocket. The last warning to come in, two hours before the collision, was from the *Mesaba*, reporting "much heavy pack ice and a great number large icebergs"; but nobody saw it because the *Titanic* operator put it under a paperweight and forgot it. Even without this ominous final message, nobody could deny—though some tried to—that the *Titanic* had been warned. Captain Smith and his officers knew they were heading into ice. . . .

Going Too Fast

On the fatal night, the *Titanic* was steaming at 21 or 22 knots. However, she was not trying to break the transatlantic speed record. In the archives of the public library of Southampton is a letter written in the 1960s by an old surviving crew member in which he says categorically that Captain Smith, urged on by the owner, J. Bruce Ismay, was trying on White Star's behalf to capture from Cunard the Blue Riband, the record for the fastest transatlantic passage by a passenger liner. This notion is and always has been absurd. No ship can go faster than another ship that is lighter and has more power, which was the relation between the *Titanic* and the crack Cunarders. At both inquiries, Ismay was closely questioned about trying to break the record and he categorically and repeatedly denied it. His indignant testimony was wholly plausible. It was simply not possible for the *Titanic* at full speed to move faster than the lighter and more powerful Cunard liners at full speed. Nor was it ever intended, either by the owners or by the builders, that the *Titanic* should be able to match them.

Many questions were asked at the inquiries about whether the *Titanic* was going flat out, or only nearly flat out, at the moment of impact. Ismay said she was not; a stoker discovered by Senator [William Alden] Smith, the chairman of the American inquiry, gave evidence to suggest that she was. The difference is unimportant. The point is that the ship was going very fast. Still more significant, both Smith and Ismay had it in mind that the ship would be tried at full speed the following day. The idea of slowing down was evidently far from their thoughts.

Experts were produced by counsel for White Star at the British inquiry who said there was nothing untoward about the *Titanic*'s speed. Other ships' captains said that Captain Smith was merely following the practice, established many years past, of maintaining course and speed in regions of ice provided that the weather was clear. But even if that was the practice, was it a safe practice? One man with experience of navigating among ice thought it dangerous and told the inquiry as much; this was Ernest Shackleton, recently returned from his first expedition to the Antarctic. He said his own custom in the vicinity of ice was to slow down to 3 or 4 knots. The lawyers defending White Star remarked that that might be so, but his own ship was very small, was it not? Naturally, Shackleton had to concede that by comparison with the *Titanic* his ship was indeed very small. But the difference in size was scarcely pertinent. The *Titanic* also was very small by comparison with the icebergs she was liable to meet and indeed did meet: 46,000 tons compared with 500,000 tons.

The [International] Ice Patrol* says that hitting such a massive though largely hidden object would have been like

---

* an organization created after the *Titanic* disaster to patrol the North Atlantic sea-lanes for ice

hitting a small island, icebergs being not only virtually indestructible but unyielding. One member of the patrol who spent three years in a U.S. Coast Guard ship in northern waters says it was their custom, when ice was in the vicinity, to proceed at no more than 3 or 4 knots. The captain of a U.S. oceanographic vessel says the same: 4 knots is fast enough. Even a "growler," the smallest sort of iceberg—defined by the Ice Patrol as being fifteen feet high or less and fifty feet long or less—should be, he says, treated with extreme care.

At the American inquiry, great hilarity was caused when Senator Smith asked Fifth Officer Harold Lowe of the *Titanic* what an ice was made of, and Lowe replied, "Ice." But the question was not quite so foolish, nor the answer quite so witty, as might at first appear. When more snow falls on a glacier, the pressure forces ice out from between the snow particles and presses in air instead. This process produces a very tight, very dense crystalline structure. The commander of the Ice Patrol said he had heard glacial ice described as "metamorphic rock," and he thought the description apt: "You could call it a mineral." With time, it gets harder. The bottom layer of the older glaciers has been estimated by carbon-dating to be some 100,000 years old; the average age of icebergs is some 3,000 years old.

Asked why, in their opinion, Captain Smith was traveling at nearly full speed when he knew he was in an ice region, the Ice Patrol says that in those days captains seem to have thought of ice and icebergs simply as one more natural hazard, like rough seas or fog. They did not instinctively regard icebergs, as any ship's captain would today, as uniquely menacing. This seems to approach the heart of the mystery. The Ice Patrol is also inclined to think that the flaw in Captain Smith's judgment was compounded by arrogance. He must have believed that the combination of his vast experience and the new technology of his ship would surmount any conceivable emergency. What he was doing on April 14, in effect, was to take his ship, at night, at speed, toward a slow-moving archipelago of rock-hard islands without even the benefit of a chart showing their approximate whereabouts.

2

The *Titanic* and Its Times: When Accountants Ruled the Waves

Roy Brander

The cause of the *Titanic* disaster has been generally known since the early hours of April 15, 1912: The ship struck an iceberg, flooded with water, and sank. But behind the simple circumstances of the wreck lay complex problems endemic to the transatlantic shipping business. According to author Roy Brander in the following selection, the White Star Line, like its competitors, gave the highest consideration to competition and profit margins, and only secondary thought to safety. The ship's designers, who assumed that the ship was as safe as modern engineering could make it, did not provide enough lifeboat space for everyone aboard, and Captain Edward Smith compounded the error by not ordering lifeboat drills. In the tragic case of the *Titanic*, confidence and acceptable risk collided with a set of extremely unlucky circumstances, dooming two-thirds of the people on board the *Titanic* to a watery grave.

The tragedy and the inquiries that followed brought about permanent changes in the operation of commercial ships. Lifeboat drills became mandatory; lifeboat space had to be provided for every passenger and every member of the crew; and a 24-hour watch was mandated for wireless rooms. Brander hails these reforms but reminds readers that such changes only come about when a tragedy such as the *Titanic*'s forces large corporations to reconsider their necessary margins of safety as well as profit.

Excerpted from "The Titanic Disaster: An Enduring Example of Money Management vs. Risk Management," by Roy Brander. Found at www.cuug.ab.ca:8001/~branderr/risk_essay/titanic.html. Reprinted with permission by the author.

When Accountants Ruled the Waves 89

I've put off starting this essay for days, because today is so appropriate. As I sit down to write, it is 11:40 P.M., April 14th, 1995. Ignoring the time zone difference, it was 83 years ago this minute that the RMS *Titanic*, on her maiden voyage in 1912, struck an iceberg. The collision was not head-on. The berg bumped and ground along the starboard side and then was gone into the calm, moonless night. At first, few thought the damage serious. It was difficult to coax passengers into the lifeboats. Yet, three hours later, the *Titanic* slammed into the ocean floor almost 4000 metres below, torn in two. Over 1500 of her passengers and crew were dead. And the design and operation of sea vessels changed dramatically and permanently.

Most of the discussion of the accident revolves around specific problems. There was the lack of sufficient lifeboats (enough for at most 1200 on a ship carrying 2200). There was the steaming ahead at full-speed despite various warnings about the ice-field. There was the lack of binoculars for the lookout. There were the poor procedures with the new invention, the wireless (not all warnings sent to the ship reached the bridge, and a nearby ship, the operator abed, missed *Titanic*'s SOS). Very recently, from recovered wreckage, "Popular Science" claimed the hull was particularly brittle even for the metallurgy of the time. (A claim now debunked.) Each has at one time or another been put forward as "THE reason the *Titanic* sank".

What gets far less comment is that most of the problems came from a larger, systemic problem: the owners and operators of steamships had for five decades taken larger and larger risks to save money—risks to which they had methodically blinded themselves. The *Titanic* disaster suddenly ripped away the blindfolds and changed dozens of attitudes, practices, and standards almost literally overnight.

The perception persists that the *Titanic* was, if obviously not "unsinkable" (though the White Star line actually never used that word in advertising), then very safe, as safe as the art could build her. That, despite various errors, the accident was mostly enormous bad luck. Nothing could be further from the truth. It was amazing good luck that there had been no similar accidents years earlier. For over 50 years, safety standards had been steadily deteriorating in various ways— almost always because of pressures to be "competitive".

Walter Lord, author of the classic "A Night to Remember", describes the process vividly in his 1986 sequel, "The Night Lives On". He compares the ships of *Titanic*'s day to the first great liner, the *Great Eastern*, built in 1858. She was designed by I.K. Brunel, England's most celebrated engineer, who got every feature he wanted. The *Great Eastern* was not the most profitable ship, but she was a triumph of safety. She had an entire inner hull two feet inside the outer. Inside that, the ship was divided by 15 transverse bulkheads, and one lengthwise into 32 compartments. Watertight lower decks further divided those. . . .

The *Titanic*'s designers thought her quite safe enough, because she could float with any two of her 16 compartments flooded, and only the worst possible accident, a collision right at a bulkhead, could even flood two. Indeed, at the bow where the ship was narrowest and the compartments much smaller, she could float with the first four flooded, and collisions were most likely at the bow.

As the *Titanic* nudged and shouldered her way past the huge iceberg, we can now estimate that a gash was torn in her almost 100 metres long. It was probably more an irregular series of holes and rips, but the cumulative area along that great length was square metres. The ship's builder, Thomas Andrews, was aboard and inspected the damage with the Captain. They found that the first five compartments were flooding rapidly, and the sixth leaking.

Andrews quickly visualized the awful, inevitable mathematics. As the front compartments filled, and the bow sank, the transverse hull [bulkhead] between the fifth and sixth compartments would drop over 10 feet—below the waterline. The water would spill over into the next compartment. So the ship would sink further, and water would spill into the next, and the next—and the pumps could only slightly delay it. The accident that nobody could imagine had occurred just that simply. Andrews underestimated her remaining time at only an hour. She lasted two.

By contrast, 50 years earlier on August 27, 1862, the *Great Eastern* had scraped on an uncharted rock off the coast of Long Island. It ripped a gash in her skin some 9 feet wide and 83 long, worse in some ways than the breach in the *Titanic*. However, the *Great Eastern*'s inner hull was unbroken and the engine room remained dry. She not only floated, but limped into New York the next day under her own steam. Not a soul was hurt.

"Defense in Depth"

Engineers today, who work in such safety-conscious designs as nuclear plants, use the military term "defense in depth". Behind the first safety system lies another, and behind that, still another . . . each with its own backups. The *Great Eastern* had defense in depth against hull breach. By the era of the *Titanic*, liners had contented themselves with but a single "layer", the all-too-short transverse bulkheads. Soon after the disaster, the sister ship *Olympic*, and many other liners with comparable designs, were being expensively retrofitted with an inner, second hull. Suddenly the "impossible costs" of such "extravagances" seemed affordable after all.

Various other corners ceased to be cut in safety standards, as well. Since all lines did the same, competitive positions remained relatively the same. (Of course, the White Star line never recovered from the loss of the *Titanic* and the settlements for cargo and loss of life; it was absorbed by Cunard lines some years later. So much for competitive advantage from trimming standards.)

The most dumbfounding cut in retrospect was the lack of lifeboats. It was not just the price of the lifeboats themselves that bothered the businessmen, it was the deck space they ate up . . . one of the most precious commodities aboard. The committee of the British Board of Trade that made the regulations on lifeboats was dominated by shipbuilders. They proved very able to convince themselves that boats for every person were not necessary. Thus the regulations of the time required only that a ship of *Titanic*'s size carry boats sufficient for 962, though she could potentially carry over 3500 passengers and crew.

White Star's General Manager Harold Sanderson pointed out that the North Atlantic was so stormy that boats could not be lowered safely 95% of the time, and even once down, the passengers would be subject to additional dangers on the tossing sea. "They could avoid all this by drowning at once" joked the magazine "Fairplay", when he continued with this view even after the accident.

Needless to say, following the disaster, complicated formulas requiring so many cubic feet of lifeboat space per thousand tons of ship were replaced with a simpler one: enough seats for everyone aboard. Again, a supposedly high cost was suddenly affordable, and has never been questioned since.

The lifeboat problem was exacerbated by poor procedure. Only at the last did lifeboats leave full; at first, many left partly empty because passengers were not queued up to them. Second Officer Herbert Lightoller took the instruction "Women and Children First" so literally that he let lifeboats leave with empty spaces rather than let men or boys as young as thirteen aboard . . . and was never so much as reprimanded for this part in seeing just over 700 saved when 1200 could have been.

For over 50 years, safety standards had been steadily deteriorating in various ways—almost always because of pressures to be "competitive".

Those of us who design and operate public services, and bear the title of "civil servant", may be much sobered by this transcript from the inquiry. Captain Maurice Henry Clarke, the inspector who cleared the *Titanic* for sailing, was being examined on the reasons for *Titanic*'s only "lifeboat drill" having been conducted at the dock, consisting of only two boats, manned by hand-picked crew. Having conceded that he had since tightened requirements, he was asked:

"Did you think your system was satisfactory before the *Titanic* disaster?"

"No, sir."

"Then why did you do it?"

"Because it was the custom."

"Do you follow a custom because it is bad?"

"Well, I am a civil servant sir, and custom guides us a good bit."

Custom still does, and not just for civil servants. A few decades ago, seat belts in cars were thought a little-needed luxury; today vastly more expensive airbags are becoming a standard feature. Those who make and sell vehicles fought the transition step-by-step as the added cost naturally reduces the number that can be afforded by the buying public. The public itself has either resigned itself to the cost, or embraced it with enthusiasm, once the statistics of death and crippling were considered. The first hockey players to use helmets were jeered by other athletes until it became the new "custom". Now most parents willingly accept the cost of helmets simply for their children to ride bicycles.

All risks need rational consideration, and some must be accepted. Sooner or later, it will be pointed out that a few head injuries occur to pedestrians, but I hope that it will never be made mandatory to wear a helmet to take a walk. Even today however, it is still often the case that money management wins out over risk management.

Sparing No Expense

What this lead to with the *Titanic* was that a lesson was only learned because the tuition was paid in blood. Has much changed? This week's news was full of the story that tractor-trailers are now being carefully examined for defects in their wheels and many pulled off the road, which costs money. This, after two people were killed by runaway wheels broken loose, both in the same week. There had been other such cases . . . but then two, close together, stimulated realization of a need for systemic change, not just a focus on the specific trucks involved.

I've been typing for hours, and my watch says it is 2:10. This is another time I recall from my *Titanic* reading. The ship went down about 2:20, and 2:10 was when her builder, Thomas Andrews, was last seen. After helping to organize the confused lifeboat loading, and personally assisting many to the last boats, he remained aboard. A survivor recalled seeing him at this time, alone in the Gentlemen's First Class Smoking Lounge, staring into space. The steward called to him to come try to swim for it, but he did not answer.

The regulations of the time required only that a ship of Titanic's *size carry [life]boats sufficient for 962, though she could potentially carry over 3500 passengers and crew.*

This room was one of the most remarkable on the ship, paneled in rich mahogany inlaid with mother-of-pearl, lit through stained glass, and even possessing a working fireplace. (No expense was spared here!) Andrews had done much of the architecture and interior design, as well as the structural and mechanical work.

I sometimes like to think that in his reverie, he realized the basic mistakes that he and a half-century of his predecessors had made. I hope it comforted him that this disaster was going to be so traumatic as to bring about tremendous changes despite all their costs, changes that would save more lives in the long run. Were it not for the *Titanic*, the safety standards might have continued for a long time, causing a long string of smaller disasters—each too small in its own right to bring about basic changes to the whole industry.

As the sinking bow lifted the stern a hundred feet in the air, *Titanic*'s own weight broke her back and ripped her in two. The enormous screaming of tons of metal tearing was a sound that haunted the survivors all their lives. I hope Andrews's thoughts had given him some sense of consolation when the hungry North Atlantic stalked into the lavish Georgian drawing room to take away his sorrow and his shame.

3
Brittle Steel May Have Contributed to the *Titanic*'s Sinking

Robert Gannon

The discovery of the *Titanic* by Robert Ballard and his crew in 1985 renewed the speculation on the causes of the *Titanic*'s sinking. The world's largest and most modern passenger ship had sunk after receiving a glancing blow from an iceberg. Was it just bad luck, or something more, that brought the ship down to the twelve-thousand-feet-deep ocean floor in about three hours?

Unfortunately for researchers, the lower starboard side of the hull was buried, preventing a look at the damage caused by the iceberg. But large fragments of the *Titanic*'s hull were recovered and brought into the laboratory for analysis. In "What Really Sank the *Titanic*," excerpted here, Robert Gannon explains the methods and findings of metallurgists who suspect that the materials used in the *Titanic*'s construction may have played a role in the ship's swift demise.

Last August, in a Canadian Department of Defense laboratory under the McDonald Bridge in Halifax, I held in my hand a discus-size piece of the hull of the *Titanic*. It had been plucked from the bottom of the sea some 500 miles southeast of the lab. Now a small team of researchers was about to cut off a section of it, a section they would try to smash.

The result, everyone hoped, would help answer a question that had been hovering for 80 years: When the *Titanic*

Reprinted from "What Really Sank the *Titanic*?" by Robert Gannon, *Popular Science*, February 1995. Reprinted with permission from Tribune Media Services.

struck that iceberg on her maiden voyage in 1912, why did she sink so fast?

Everyone by now knows the *Titanic*'s story: the largest ship in the world, built by a work force of 17,000, the ultimate in turn-of-the-century design and technology. First-class suites ran to more than $55,000 in today's dollars, and when she sailed on her maiden voyage from Southampton, England, en route to New York, she held among her 2,227 passengers the cream of industrial society, including, for instance Colonel John Jacob Astor, Macy's founder and U.S. Congressman Isidor Straus, and Thomas Andrews, the ship's builder.

The ship was luxurious and it was safe—virtually unsinkable—for it was built of easily sealed-off compartments. If, for some unimaginable reason, the hull were punctured, only the compartment actually ruptured would flood. In a worst-case situation—two ships ramming each other for example—builders figured that the *Titanic* would take from one to three days to sink, time for nearby ships to help.

But things didn't work out that way.

"Iceberg Dead Ahead!"

Start on that April evening at about 7:30, at the first ominous hint of disaster. Into the earphones of the wireless operator on duty came a message from the steamer *California[n]* an hour or so away: *Three Large Bergs Five Miles Southward From Us.* But the *Titanic* continued to rush through the deepening darkness. High in the crow's nest, two lookouts shivered as they peered ahead into the gloom. The temperature was one degree above freezing.

Had there been a moon, they would have seen ice floes already off to the sides. Had there been a wind, foam from waves breaking against the ice would have shown up misty-white in the starlight. But the sky was dark, the sea dead flat.

Just after 11:30, the *Titanic* was 95 miles south of the Grand Banks of Newfoundland. Lookout Frederic Fleet, squinting into the dark, noticed the horizon directly ahead becoming less clear, slightly hazy. The stars began to wink out. And then he began to make out a black mountain. "Iceberg dead ahead!" he shouted, and quickly rang the wheelhouse.

The officer in charge immediately signaled "full speed astern" to the engine room, and directed the wheelman to turn hard to port.

The crow's nest lookouts braced themselves for collision. But slowly the ship began to turn. The iceberg passed the bow and moved along the starboard side.

A wall of ice, as one report put it, "like a windjammer with sails the color of wet canvas," moved past the railing as chunks from it fell onto deck. Some passengers grabbed pieces to cool their drinks. Those who looked out their portholes were baffled by the dark mass gliding by.

A Sound Like Breaking China

The ice struck with not much more than a jar—certainly not hard enough for worry—and in seconds it had disappeared into the darkness astern. But down in a sweltering boiler room near the bow, a geyser of water was drenching stokers as they leapt through a quickly closing watertight door. In the next compartment too, water was gushing through the hull.

The ice struck with not much more than a jar—certainly not hard enough for worry—and in seconds it had disappeared into the darkness astern.

When *Titanic* builder Andrews assessed the damage—the iceberg had pierced the first six watertight compartments—he realized the seriousness of the great ship's condition. Grimly, he gave Captain Edward Smith the bad news. Smith reluctantly agreed to evacuate the *Titanic*, for both men foresaw the awful drama to come: When the ruptured compartments filled with sea water, the extra weight would make the ship pitch forward. Though the cubicles were called "watertight" in fact they weren't. Their tops were open, their walls extending only a few feet above the waterline. Because of the *Titanic*'s nose-down tilt as each compartment filled, it would spill over to the next. They were watertight only horizontally. Nobody expected the water to rise above the waterline.

As open portholes disappeared beneath the surface, water flooded through them, adding to the deluge, and the pitch worsened. The propellers lifted free, and from inside the ship came a sound like breaking china. Then, great rumblings—perhaps the shifting of the five grand pianos or hundreds of trunks. And suddenly, with a screech of tearing metal, the forward funnel buckled over into the ocean.

The first lifeboat had touched the sea at 12:45. But all the lifeboats combined could accommodate little more than half of the passengers. At just before 2:00 in the morning, with the ship upended to about 45 degrees and the bow no longer visible, those in the lifeboats heard a deep rumbling. The stern began to settle, but then it tilted up again, the forward part slipping downward, pulled down, postmortem speculation went, by the water-filled bow.

Exploring the Damage

At 2:20, the *Titanic* slipped beneath the surface, carrying with her more than 1,500 passengers. The largest movable object ever built, designed to take at least three days to sink in case of the worst-imaginable catastrophe, settled to her grave in less than three hours.

The reason, engineers guessed over the years, was that nobody foresaw the massive sideswiping damage a piece of ice the size of a high-rise could do. The berg must have pushed in the ten-by-30-foot steel plates, they speculated, popping the rivets and pulling them apart at the seams to let the water gush through.

But the math didn't add up. Not when those likely gaps at the edges of the plates were correlated with reports of damage noted by seamen before the ship went down. And not with the speed of sinking. The submergence equation needed some other unknown.

For nearly three-quarters of a century, that's all anyone knew—until oceanographer Bob Ballard, in September 1985, found the wreck of the *Titanic* at a depth of 12,612 feet. He was surprised to discover that the ship lay in two sections—stern and bow—separated by a wide field of debris. His remote cameras tried to spy the gash left by the iceberg—but that part of the bow was buried in an 85-foot-deep mud bank, plowed up as the *Titanic* hit bottom.

Six more years passed, and in 1991 the first (and so far only) purely scientific team visited the site; other groups have been primarily exploratory. Leading the scientists was Steve Blasco, a 48-year-old ocean-floor geologist with Canada's Department of Natural Resources. Graybearded, skin weathered by saltspray, he looks every bit the seasoned sailor—he even walks like one—and he loves the sea.

Blasco's team was part of what was called the Imax dive, because the expedition's principal purpose was to generate a 70-mm-format film for the six-story screens of Imax theaters. The research and filmmaking dives were made in a pair of Soviet *Mir* submersibles capable of staying down 20 hours, using 110,000-lumen lamps originally developed for filming *The Abyss*.

While the Imax photographers shot their $8-million film, Blasco and his people pursued the science. "We don't know much about this depth, this continental rise," says Blasco, "neither the geology nor the biology. And we certainly don't know anything about the interaction of a ship and the ocean floor that deep." Most ships sink in water that is shallow; those that don't are rarely found.

The *Titanic* Tomb

The *Titanic* was brand-new when she sank. That makes her a singular measuring device, a "historic marker" Blasco calls her, a notch in time revealing the rate of natural activity—what has happened on the ocean floor over the 80 years until her discovery, and what will happen in the future.

The Titanic *was brand-new when she sank. That makes her a singular measuring device, a "historic marker" . . . a notch in time revealing the rate of natural activity.*

In the tomb that was once a ship, all that remain are china teacups and brass latches, porcelain toilets and perhaps teeth—nearly all else has been devoured: wooden decks, the rich Victorian woodwork, human beings, their clothing—all except for shoes protected from scavengers by their tannin. (Some 150 items retrieved by the French sub *Nautile* went on display at London's National Maritime Museum in October 1994.)

Protected too is the ship's steel; corrosion, to everyone's surprise, is nearly absent (a fact of interest to companies working with pipelines or cables).

On the last dive of the trip, one of the *Mirs* came across a chunk of metal that looked like a part of the hull. The scientists had agreed beforehand that they would bring up no human artifacts; they felt that the site should be consecrated as a burial ground, and that retrieval of personal items would smack of grave robbing. But for strictly scientific purposes, they did want to bring up a sample of the hull.

And there it was, resting on a ripple of ocean-floor silt as though placed there the previous month: a Frisbee-size chunk an inch thick, with three rivet holes, each an inch and a quarter across. Back aboard the mother ship, with surface grime carefully squirted off the piece with a high-pressure water jet, researchers were surprised to see remnants of the original paint.

By now, that piece of steel should have corroded nearly to oblivion. But when a metallurgist saw it later, he had an immediate explanation: "Of course—there's no oxygen down there." Then Blasco pointed out that fish were swimming about, and the metallurgist stopped talking.

So how could there have been so little corrosion? It somehow involves temperature and pressure," says Blasco, "That's not a very good explanation, but it's all we have for now."

Of even more interest to those intrigued by the question of the ship's unseemly rapid sinking was the condition of the edges of the hull piece: jagged, almost shattered. And the metal itself showed no evidence of bending. High-quality ship steel, metallurgists know, has a lot more give, more ductility, than most people imagine, and probably wouldn't break. Yet the edges of this sample looked almost as though they were made of broken china.

Metallurgical Research

Three years later, now, in the Halifax testing lab, I pick up that hunk of the *Titanic* from a work table. It's been sitting among broken gears, split I-beams, and ruptured flanges from other ships, representing various naval problems, and it looks like junk. I remind myself that it's the only one of its kind in the world. The 80-year-old paint is splotchy-brown, with an underlying smear of lead oxide, now pinkish-orange.

One edge is ruler-straight and shiny where a strip of metal has been sliced off. A few test pieces, cigarette-size "coupons," have been fashioned from the strip. Some have already been destroyed in preliminary testing in another government laboratory in Ottawa. The last piece will soon be mounted in a device that will conduct what is called a

Brittle Steel May Have Contributed to Sinking

Charpy test. In the lab are Blasco and another of the Imax team, Duncan Ferguson, a 34-year-old mechanical engineer.

The metallurgist in charge is Ken KarisAllen, 35, a government specialist in cracks and corrosion. He's energetic, quick moving, almost taut, and when he speaks of his Charpy machine, he does so with fondness.

A Charpy tests brittleness, he explains, nonchalantly pushing the machine's huge pendulum. Testing is simple: As a coupon [sample] is held tightly against a steel holder, the pendulum—67 pounds and 2½ feet long—swings down and thumps against the sample, sometimes breaking it. The pendulum's point of contact is instrumented, with a readout of forces electronically recorded in millisecond detail.

KarisAllen will test two coupons; one, a sample of a standard, good quality steel used in modern ships; the other, the slice from the *Titanic*. "If things go as I foresee," he says, "the first piece will go 'thud.' The second will tinkle."

Both coupons are resting in a bath of alcohol at -1°C—to simulate the water temperature of 80 years ago. KarisAllen must rush the test piece from the bath to the holder in five seconds.

He hauls the weight up and locks it in place. "OK?" he asks, and looks around the room. "Here goes."

With a pair of stainless-steel tongs, he lifts the first coupon from the bath and whisks it to the holder, reaches quickly to the red release handle, and yanks. The pendulum swings down and thuds to a halt. The test piece has been bent into a "V."

Now he repeats the procedure with the *Titanic* sample.

This time there is no thump. The pendulum strikes the piece with a sharp ping, barely slows, and continues up on its swing while the sample, broken in two, sails across the room to smack a metal wastebasket.

Tracings on the computer screen confirm what the metallurgists suspected, and now have seen: the *Titanic*'s hull steel is brittle. When it met the iceberg, the hull plates didn't simply bend in. They fractured.

The steel is embrittled not from sitting on the ocean floor for most of a century. It was that way when it came from the steel plant, and it became even more brittle slicing through that 29°F water. "To make present-day high-quality steel that brittle," says KarisAllen, "I'd have to lower its temperature to -60 or -70°C."

Brittle Fracture

"Back then nobody understood the concept of brittle fracture," adds Ferguson. "They tested the steel for tensile strength [the maximum stress a material can withstand before it breaks], and if it passed, that was that." What they didn't know then was that high sulfur content makes for brittleness, and *Titanic* steel was high even for the times. "It's full of sulfide occlusions called 'stringers,' and it would never get out of the yard today. It wouldn't even make good rebar, which is pretty lousy steel." Blasco breaks in: "Shipbuilding technology had outstripped metallurgy technology." He sounds as though he's had that thought before.

> *"Back then nobody understood the concept of brittle fracture."*

Even if the builders had known the steel was brittle, they still wouldn't have worried. The ship's design, they believed, would guard against calamities. But of course they were wrong.

William Garzke, a senior naval architect with the New York firm of Gibbs & Cox, has taken all the data gathered on the sinking, and using forensic procedures has developed a scenario of what happened on that night in 1912. Ferguson (the only mechanical engineer to be part of any of the six *Titanic* expeditions) has studied the sequence, too, concentrating on events beneath the surface.

Combine those scenarios with half a dozen others (along with the eyewitness accounts of the sinking), and you have this likely sequence:

11:35 p.m., April 14, 1912. Up in the crow's nest, the lookouts spot the iceberg a quarter-mile ahead—and that's too bad. Had they not alerted the bridge, the ship would not have attempted a turn; it would have rammed the iceberg head on. Damage would have been limited mostly to two or three compartments; it would have caused almost no pitch, certainly not enough to pull the compartments below the waterline. Many injuries would have resulted—after all, the ship would have crashed into the 200,000-ton ice mountain traveling at 26 mph, and crew members were sleeping in the forepeak. But the *Titanic* wouldn't have sunk.

11:40. The ship sideswipes the ice. Were the one-inch-thick hull made of modern, relatively ductile steel, certainly

Brittle Steel May Have Contributed to Sinking 103

it would have bent, stretched, and broken in plastic deformation, popping loose rivets, pulling apart at the seams, cracking the caulking and allowing water to pour in. But because of the steel's ductility, it would have absorbed massive amounts of energy. The ship might have quickly slowed, or even bounced away.

Some of that does happen. But the ice also crashes right through the plating as it grinds along the side, striking at an angle perfect for the most destruction, tearing the plates, cracking and splitting the hull below and above the waterline like a 300-foot zipper.

Cracks in the brittle steel now propagate rapidly. They run like lightning strokes to the plate edges, stopping only where the plates are riveted together.

(In post-disaster hearings, the few survivors who saw the water enter didn't report it squirting in through the seams. They described it as a water wall. Some of the ten-by-30-foot plates, in fact, may have been wholly cracked off. But that evidence lies buried in ocean-floor mud. Had the builders guarded against steel embrittlement, the vessel most likely would have stayed afloat long enough for other ships in the vicinity to arrive for rescue.)

Midnight. Those first six compartments are filling; water is beginning to slosh over.

12:40 a.m. Water aboard now equals 453 cubic meters—enough to fill 2,000 bathtubs.

1:20. The bow dips; water floods through anchor-chain holds. Absent those watertight compartments, incoming water would have been spreading out, and the ship would be settling on an even keel—and probably still be afloat for another six hours.

2:00. The bow continues to submerge; three mammoth propellers lift free; the stack topples.

2:10. The *Titanic* tilts to 45 degrees or more. The bending moment [pressure] on the midships is immense, for a portion of the ship the size of a 25-story building hangs unsupported. Stress reaches nearly 15 tons per square inch.

Suddenly, at a point at or just beneath the surface, the topside pulls apart, while the hull girder near the ship's center fails. The keel bends; the bottom plating buckles.

As the frigid seawater floods into the ships's bowels, says Garzke, there is "a spectacular failure, with the steel of the upper structure fragmenting all over the place." The deep rumbling heard by those in lifeboats is probably not caused by failing equipment, but by fracturing steel.

2:12. The stern angles high above the water; the bow, dangling beneath, fills with water, grows heavier and heavier until it reaches some 16,000 tons of water in weight, and . . .

2:18. The bow rips loose. Free from that weight, the stern rises sharply (at least one lifeboat passenger says, "Look—its coming back!"), holds an almost vertical position, and then, as it fills, fades downward again.

2:20. Almost gently, the stern slides beneath the surface.

The bow, meanwhile has been coasting down at a maximum of about 13 mph (a figure based both on Ferguson's hydrodynamic calculations and those of soils engineer Bill Roggensack of Canada's Centre for Frontier Engineering Research, working with data from bottom sediment plowed up along a 35-foot-high path by the bow.)

Beginning perhaps 100 feet below the surface, sections of the stern still holding air succumb to water pressure. The spaces implode, scattering tons of material through the water.

2:29. The bow strikes the bottom, 12,612 feet down, angling downward and plowing into the mud.

2:56. The stern, having fallen nearly vertically at about four mph, crashes—nearly 36 minutes after submerging—two-fifths of a mile from the bow.

Impact of the *Titanic*

It hits rudder first. The impact rips the propeller shaftings from the hull, leaving the propellers on the seabed as the keel sinks in. Two deck cranes break loose from their mountings, thrown backward and peeling back the poop deck. They come to rest 40 feet aft of the stern. Debris will rain down for hours.

The many lessons learned from the *Titanic* changed the way maritime companies thought about lifeboats, communications, and ship design. But one lesson was not well learned—that construction technology shouldn't be allowed to outrun materials science. Just because something can be built doesn't mean it should be.

That is what the Canadians mean when they call the *Titanic* "the 1912 *Challenger*," after the ill-fated space shuttle. Both disasters resulted from a failure to understand how a material—whether brittle steel plate or brittle rubber steel—would behave.

4

Captain Smith Inadvertently Sank the *Titanic*

David G. Brown

Author David G. Brown undertook a four-year study of the facts surrounding the sinking of the *Titanic* and came to the conclusion that many of the commonly accepted notions of the event must be not only wrong, but impossible. First, the physics of ship maneuvering prevented the sideswiping collision of the *Titanic* with an iceberg—one of the details of the tragedy that has been agreed upon by every writer and movie director who ever attempted to tell the *Titanic* story. Rather than a side collision, which would have knocked hundreds of people off their feet, the *Titanic* must have ground across the top of a submerged ice shelf, an occurrence that explains why the survivors all reported nothing more than a slight jarring or rumbling deep within the ship.

Brown saves his most damning theories for Captain Edward Smith. It was the captain's decision to restart the engines a few minutes after the collision and make for Halifax, the nearest port, that actually sunk the ship. Until that order was issued, the ship's pumps were successfully dealing with the water flowing into the lower holds and boiler rooms—the *Titanic* would have remained afloat if only it had remained still. After the ship got underway, however, its forward momentum allowed water to rush into the *Titanic* at a much faster rate. The *Titanic* was damaged by natural forces, but destroyed by human error.

Excerpted from "The Last Log of the Titanic," by David G. Brown. From the Encyclopedia Titanica website found at www.encyclopedia-titanica.org/articles/lastlog_brown. Reprinted with permission.

The Last Log of the Titanic is not intended for readers who believe in impossible shipboard romances or giant blue gems. Nor is it for anyone seeking to rewrite history with lurid flights of imagination. *The Last Log of the* Titanic is a serious attempt to unravel the events on *Titanic*'s bridge and in its engine rooms that led to the accident and the ship's eventual foundering. To do that, I spent four years researching original sources—mostly the 1912 testimony of the crew who survived. There are no new "discoveries" in this book. The facts it contains were put into the public record in 1912. However, what I discovered is that the real story of *Titanic* is totally different from the official myths pushed onto a gullible public nearly 90 years ago. As usual, the truth is far more compelling than myth and legend.

This project started out as part of an article on boat handling for *Boating World* magazine. My intention was to use the scene from the then-popular movie which showed *Titanic*'s starboard bow grazing the iceberg to illustrate how boats do NOT maneuver. It is impossible for a rudder-steered vessel to damage only its starboard bow as depicted in the movie during a left turn. This is because of the location of the pivot point around which the hull rotates during a turn. If *Titanic* had struck the berg as shown on the movie screen, damage would have occurred to its entire starboard side, not just the bow.

Murdoch's "Port Around"

We know that after Lookout [Frederick] Fleet's final iceberg warning, Second Officer William Murdoch initially ordered the ship to turn to its left (starboard helm in 1912). *Titanic* undoubtedly turned slightly faster to the left than to the right because it was driven by three propellers. Every propeller delivers both forward thrust and sideways pressure. A propeller that rotates to the left in forward also pushes the stern to the left. Conversely, a propeller that rotates to the right pushes the stern to the right when the ship is moving forward. Two of *Titanic*'s propellers rotated to the right, giving the ship a slight tendency to swing its stern to the right (turning the bow to the left) when steaming forward. This meant the ship turned a bit faster to the left (starboard helm in 1912) than to the right. By ordering a left turn, Murdoch took advantage of the ship's natural tendency.

Virtually every report, book, TV documentary and motion picture has depicted *Titanic* sideswiping its starboard bow on the iceberg while turning left, away from danger. Not only did this not happen, but it could not have happened under any circumstances. A starboard bow sideswipe "collision" while turning left was impossible for a conventional ship in 1912. (Nor can it be done today.) The manner in which rudder-steered ships pivot in the water does not allow the actual damage received by *Titanic*'s bow to have occurred during a left turn. Iceberg damage to the starboard bow while turning to the left absolutely would have necessitated bumping and grinding of the ice along the ship's starboard side all the way to its stern.

Every conventional power-driven vessel has a "pivot point" located on its centerline roughly one-third of its length aft from the bow. The vessel rotates around this point when its rudder is put over. Because the pivot point is not amidships but is offset toward the bow, the vessel's stern swings a larger arc than the bow. Turning only to the left (or right) [to] avoid a close-aboard object swings the vessel's stern toward that object even though the bow points clear. A side-on impact cannot be avoided. The object then bumps and grinds along the side of the ship doing damage along the entire length of the hull from the initial point of impact to the stern.

The impossible "left turn only" scenario would have caused damage to the majority of the ship's 16 primary watertight compartments. The truth is, *Titanic* did not receive ice damage aft of Boiler Room #5 which was approximately below the bridge. This is proof the ship was turning to the right at the time of the accident, turning toward the iceberg.

Immediately following the accident, Murdoch told Captain Smith that he attempted to "port around" the deadly berg. This maneuver for dodging an obstacle is familiar to every mariner. The bow is first turned away from the object, then the helm is shifted (turned the other way) to clear the stern. That is exactly what Murdoch must have done, because the ship did not suffer any ice damage aft of Boiler Room #5. In truth, the bow was clear of the ice until Murdoch executed his second turn, back toward the berg. This second turn was not a mistake. Even though the bow had been pointed away from the ice, *Titanic*'s stern was sliding dangerously toward the berg when Murdoch shifted the helm. Only when he initiated a turn to the right did the fragile stern swing away from the iceberg and certain disaster.

Murdoch's "port around" maneuver required the ship to be extremely close to the berg before initiating the second turn. As a result, the iceberg would have appeared to be off the starboard bow when Murdoch called for port helm to turn the ship to the right. Quartermaster [Alfred] Olliver apparently was fooled by the angle of the ship to berg when he said Murdoch's port helm order came after the berg passed the bridge. "The iceberg was away up astern," he told Senator [Theodore] Burton at the U.S. hearings.

If *Titanic* had been turning left (starboard helm in 1912) at the moment of contact, ice and metal should have met roughly in the way of the bulkhead between Boiler Rooms #5 and #6. In reality, this is about the location on the hull where damage from the ice ended. In the mythical left turn, the berg would have bumped and crashed along the ship's entire starboard side starting at Boiler Room #5 and continuing aft into Boiler Rooms #4, #3, #2, #1 and the two engine rooms. Compartments forward of Boiler Room #5 would have remained undamaged and free of water. *Titanic* still would have foundered, but stern first. Of course, the pattern of damage to be expected during a left turn collision is exactly the opposite to what actually occurred.

The timing of Murdoch's second turn in his "port around" maneuver, the one back toward the danger, was critical. Unfortunately, he started his turn a bit too soon and the bow came a few yards too close to the berg. Actual damage received by the starboard bow during the accident is irrefutable proof that *Titanic* was under port helm and turning to the right (starboard) at the moment of impact. Murdoch did, in fact, "port around" the portion of the berg above the water. . . .

Having found the conventional story of the accident is physically impossible, I began a quest to learn if any other commonly-believed details of the accident were wrong. That took me on a nearly four-year adventure through testimony from hearings on both sides of the Atlantic as well as into the dusty archives of libraries. What I uncovered astounded me because, at the time, I still believed the conventional story of the isolated iceberg, the failed left turn, the engines pounding in reverse, and the ship remaining stopped until it sank.

Myth and Legend

Late at night I often found myself too excited to sleep as *Titanic*'s crew spoke to me through their 1912 testimony. Time after time I would suspect a quartermaster, fireman or lookout of lying—only to find overwhelming evidence supporting those claims. It became obvious to me that the events experienced by the crew were not those etched into history by either the U.S. Senate or the British Board of Trade inquiry.

According to Fourth Officer [Joseph] Boxhall, First Officer Murdoch changed the orders to the two outboard propellers from AHEAD FULL to ASTERN FULL, requesting what sailors call a "crash stop." This is a violent maneuver that can damage the ship's engines, drive shafts, or propellers. For that reason, it is reserved only for the worst of emergencies. Testifying in London, Boxhall said the engine order telegraphs read "full speed astern" when he stepped into the enclosed section of the bridge.

Unfortunately Boxhall's recollection seems faulty. *Titanic* never attempted the crash stop that people on land still believe was the obvious way to prevent the ship from slamming into the iceberg. Reverse thrust from the propellers would have eliminated the ability of the single rudder to steer the ship. Murdoch knew this. Under full reverse power the ship could not have pivoted to the right, but would have begun a sideways slide into the iceberg.

The toil of those sweaty men feeding the fires in the ship's boiler rooms was [accompanied] by red warning lights and clanging bells moments before the accident. "Shut the dampers," sang out Leading Stoker Frederick Barrett. He and Second Engineer James H. Hesketh had been talking in Boiler Room #6 when the alarms clanged and the lights on the stoking indicators changed from white to red. Chatter among the men stopped in mid-sentence as they turned to this unexpected work. Closing the dampers on the furnaces was an ordinary precaution to reduce the fires to prevent generating excess steam pressure while the engineers stopped the engines. There were safety valves, of course, but these were not foolproof and had been known to stick on occasion. Nobody wanted to risk building up excessive steam pressure.

The command to close the dampers came just prior to impact when *Titanic* was perhaps 700 feet from the berg.

Closing the furnace dampers is yet another indication that a crash stop was never performed. Full reverse power would have required as much steam as possible from the boilers. Shutting the dampers would have been the worst possible thing to do during a crash stop. Instead, stokers would have been asked to rake the coals in their furnaces to increase steam output from the boilers in order to get maximum power out of the engines.

Titanic's engines and associated drive shafts and propeller blades were designed to withstand an instant shift from forward into reverse at harbor speeds. They might have had strength enough to withstand the strain of instant reversal at 22.5 knots, but only if every part from cylinder to tail shaft was totally free of defects. Ships have been known to snap shafts and propeller blades during crash stops. If nothing broke on *Titanic*, a crash stop would have caused a rumbling shudder to convulse through the after third of the hull. . . .

Since none of the seven-hundred *Titanic* survivors described such a memorable event, and because the firebox dampers were ordered shut, the engineers could not have performed a crash stop. They just closed the throttles to the engines to stop them from pushing the liner forward. In sailor terms, *Titanic* was "shooting," or coasting forward without power when it contacted the iceberg.

Fatal Contact

Where was the fatal ice damage done to the ship? "To the side," history has answered for 88 years—despite both the physical impossibility of such damage and the direct testimony to the contrary by members of the crew. Scenes in the movies show the starboard bow of the giant liner slamming against a wall of ice much like an automobile sideswiping a highway bridge abutment. Nothing could be further from the truth. If the ship had collided with the berg in that manner, the impact would have been devastating. Men sleeping in the bow would have been thrown out of their bunks to the hard steel decks. Anyone standing in the grand First Class entrance likely would have had their feet knocked from beneath them. Certainly there would have been dozens (if not scores) of injuries: broken arms, legs and even skulls. More than a few people would have been killed outright as the steel bow collapsed around them.

With full right rudder (port helm in 1912) *Titanic* was turning to the right as it contacted the ice. There had been those few quick seconds when it appeared the daring S-curve would succeed. However, as every child learns in school, the bulk of an iceberg lies beneath the water. Murdoch knew it, too. He fully expected what happened next. *Titanic*'s fragile underbelly scraped across an underwater shelf called an "ice ram." These shelves are common enough to warrant special attention in Bowditch*. "It is dangerous to approach close to an iceberg of any size because of the possibility of encountering underwater extensions," the navigation text cautions. The great danger of icebergs is "underwater extensions, called rams, which are usually formed due to the more intensive melting or erosion of the unsubmerged portion."

> *Scenes in the movies show the starboard bow of the giant liner slamming against a wall of ice much like an automobile sideswiping a highway bridge abutment. Nothing could be further from the truth.*

Physical evidence and eyewitness accounts point to the accident being a grounding, not a collision. *Titanic* did not run into an iceberg; it ran over an iceberg. The initial pattern of flooding and testimony from surviving crew members are consistent on one point: the bottom of the ship—not the side—made solid contact with the ice. Survivors unanimously described the sound and vibration of a ship running aground. There was no sharp jolt of a ship slamming horizontally into an immovable object. Instead, the slight tremble was barely enough to rattle silverware set out for breakfast in the First Class dining saloon.

The difference between a grounding and a collision is far more significant than it appears. Head-on impact with the berg would have sent all of *Titanic*'s 52,310 displacement tons smashing into the ice at a speed of almost 36 feet per second. In the crunch of a head-on impact, the ship's speed would have effectively dropped to zero. Everything inside the bow that was not tied down—people, chairs, bottles of

---

*American navigator Nathaniel Bowditch (1773–1838) wrote *The American Practical Navigator*, a standard reference book for sailors.

wine, soup tureens—everything would have continued moving. Sleeping immigrant men near the bow would have been sent flying out of their bunks. Farther aft, the impact would have been less, but still substantial. Women could have been hurled down the grand staircase in First Class to land twisted and broken in a pile of taffeta. In the Second Class smoking room behind the fourth funnel men might have felt their chairs move beneath them.

Edward Wilding, one of the naval architects who designed *Titanic*, testified in London about the effect of a head-on collision. "If she struck a fair blow I think we should have heard a great deal more about the severity of it, and probably the ship would have come into harbor," he said. "I am afraid she would have killed every fireman down in the firemen's quarters, but I feel sure the ship would come in." At the U.S. Senate hearings Captain John J. Knapp, the U.S. Navy's hydrographer, tried to imagine such an impact for Senator William Alden Smith:

> MR. KNAPP: . . . an idea may be formed as to the possible blow by using the accepted formula, the weight multiplied by the square of the velocity divided by twice the gravity. Multiplying . . . will give the blow that would have been struck if she had kept straight on her course against this apparently solid mass of ice, which, at a speed of 21 knots, would have been equal to 1,173,200 foot tons, or energy enough to lift 14 monuments the size of the Washington Monument in one second of time.
>
> —U.S. Senate Hearings
> May 18, 1912

Naval architect Wilding raised an interesting point about a head-on accident involving an extremely large ship. The bow of *Titanic* would have crumpled much like the "crumple zone" of a modern automobile. Crumpling would have absorbed much of the force of the blow by spreading it out over time. According to Wilding, telescoping of the ship in this manner would have reduced injuries among the passengers and crew who were lucky enough not to have been trapped in crumpled sections of the bow.

While less dramatic, the more often invoked "glancing blow" at 22.5 knots would have created its own kind of havoc. At impact, the deck would have jumped sideways relative to anything not rivetted to it. This "rebound effect" should have been as disruptive to people living in the forward third of the ship as a major earthquake in a large hotel ashore: sleeping Third Class passengers tossed to the hard steel decks; personal items tumbled off shelves; people thrown down. There would have been fewer injuries and less spilled drinks than during a head-on collision, but some deaths and broken bones. Either type of horizontal impact—head-on or glancing blow—would have been unforgettable from the point of view of a passenger. None of the more than 700 survivors remembered as dramatic as either a head-on or "glancing blow" impact happening.

What a sailor calls "rebound" is known scientifically as "impulse and momentum." These are the words naval architect Bill Garzke used to explain the traditional bow sideswipe. . . . He envisioned the hull striking the ice, then rebounding to strike again . . . and again . . . for nearly 300 feet along the bow. Garzke's description of events may have been inspired by Lightoller who described essentially the same type of accident in his autobiography.

> The impact flung her bow off, but only by the whip or spring of the ship. Again she struck, this time a little further aft. Each blow stove in a plate, below the water line, as the ship had not the inherent strength to resist.
>
> —Charles H. Lightoller
> *Titanic and Other Ships*, 1935

Striking the Ground

Alternatively, a single hard sideswipe of the iceberg might have caused enough crumpling of the ship's hull to have cushioned the blow. In this impact the bending, twisting and shattering of steel would have produced a single huge hole at the point of contact with no damage anywhere else. Of course, *Titanic* did not receive damage to only one spot on the bow. Damage extended over a distance of nearly 250 feet from the forepeak all the way into Boiler Room #5. It is the extended nature of this damage that argues most effectively against the "impulse and momentum" type of rebounding impact.

More to the point, the theory of multiple impacts does not fit the experiences described by survivors. Each impulse and rebound would have whipped the deck sideways beneath the feet of passengers and crew. That is not the type of impact anyone reported. The universal description of the accident was a rumbling or vibration, not side-to-side motion of the deck.

Rapid horizontal motion of a deck knocks people off their feet much quicker than a large roll of the ship. This is because friction keeps the person's feet in place on the deck when it jerks sideways. The victim's torso has inertia which resists sideways movement, with the result that the feet move out from beneath the individual's body. The person's center of gravity is suddenly and unexpectedly no longer supported in a straight line by the legs. A fall is almost inevitable.

If the Lightoller/Garzke horizontal impact took place, an indelible memory of a large percentage of surviving Third Class men who happened to be standing upright in their cabins near the bow would have been an unexpected tumble to the deck. Crew members in their quarters at the very front of the ship would have had the same disquieting experience. Instead, except for one man, they universally recalled only a slight trembling as the ship passed over the ice.

Soft or hard, a grounding is exactly what passengers and crew aboard Titanic *experienced during the seven seconds when the ship was in contact with the ice.*

When a ship "strikes the ground," the action can be quite stately. Speed often drops gradually, so gradually that the first moments of a grounding go unnoticed even by professional seamen. Sliding onto mud or sand may produce almost no sound or vibration. Striking on a hard surface can sound like pouring marbles over sheet metal. Neither type of grounding is the smashing impact of iron against an immovable object. Soft or hard, a grounding is exactly what passengers and crew aboard *Titanic* experienced during the seven seconds when the ship was in contact with the ice.

Author Lawrence Beesley, a teacher on his way to America for holiday, was in Cabin D-56 just aft of the Second Class dining saloon when the ship slid over the ice. His personal experience is a perfect illustration of a ship going aground, not colliding head-on:

> ... there came what seemed to me nothing more than an extra heave of the engines and a more than usually obvious dancing motion of the mattress on which I sat. Nothing more than that—no sound of a crash or anything else: no sense of shock, no jar that felt like one heavy body meeting another.

— Lawrence Beesley, *The Loss of The S.S. Titanic, Its Story and Its Lessons*, Houghton Mifflin, 1912

A grounding such as Beesley described is soft because it does not take place in an instant. Only a small portion of the vessel's displacement weight is involved at the beginning. That increases as the ship slides onto the ground, but this increase is spread over time. The event is not instantaneous like a head-on collision, but takes several seconds from first touch until the ship either stops or breaks free.

Ice on the Deck

A full-size iceberg has hundreds of times more mass than *Titanic*. Each cubic yard of berg is roughly a ton of solid ice. The ship was a hollow metal structure filled mostly with air. In a head-on collision, there would not have been enough time for the energy of *Titanic* to overcome the inertia of the ice and push the berg sideways. But, the ship didn't hit the berg. It spent those seven seconds grinding across the top of an underwater ice shelf. There was plenty of time for the berg to move a bit under the ship's weight. Ice felt the ship as much as the ship felt the ice, and the berg rolled ever so slightly toward *Titanic*.

It rolled because icebergs are notoriously unstable. Just as Captain Smith told his New York friends, the upper part extending into the atmosphere melts at a different rate from the underwater portions. This upsets the equilibrium of a berg, which often compensates by suddenly capsizing. "Icebergs that are in the process of disintegrating may suddenly capsize or readjust their masses," warns Bowditch. When the ship rode onto the shelf, the berg was forced to support increasing tons of steel, rivets and passengers well outboard of its center of gravity. Like any other floating object, the berg tipped toward this extra weight.

As it tipped, the upper portions of the berg brushed against the ship's topsides at the forward end of the well deck. This contact precipitated the famous mini-avalanche of ice. Brushing against the top of the berg probably didn't scratch the liner's fresh paint. During the middle 1990s, scientists studied the impact of icebergs against iron or steel objects. This research was aimed at developing offshore oil rigs for use on the Grand Banks near the spot where *Titanic* now lies. Experiments have shown that ice above a berg's waterline can be relatively soft and often crumbles upon impact. Crumbling produced the broken pieces of ice that littered the ship's forward well deck.

"There was quite a lot of ice on the starboard part of the ship," 26-year-old Olaus Abelseth told the U.S. investigation. The young Norwegian was sleeping in the Third Class open berthing area on Lower Deck G near the bow of the ship. Also near the bow was Frank O. Evans, a 27-year-old Able Seaman. "I was sitting at the table reading a book, and all of a sudden I felt a slight jar," he testified in New York. "I did not take any notice of it for a few minutes until one of the other able seamen came down with a big lump of ice in his hands.". . .

Under Way for Halifax

Fatal damage did not necessarily mean sudden death for *Titanic* as the British report implied. There is evidence from the ship's Chief Engineer that the pumps were successful in slowing the flooding of Boiler Room #6 during the first ten minutes after the accident. Pumping definitely was able to keep even with the inrush of water into Boiler Room #5. This is not to suggest that the ship would have floated indefinitely, only that *Titanic* might have floated as long as there was bunker coal to keep its pumps running. The ship could not founder until Boiler Room #6 was lost. That does not appear to have been imminent as late as 11:50 P.M., thanks to the pumps.

A basic precept of safe navigation is to never make assumptions, especially assumptions based on scanty information. Ismay and Smith assumed their ship was safe to steam again based on Boxhall's visit to the Third Class berths and scanty information about the extent of damage and the ability of the pumps to cope with the flooding. *Titanic* was more seriously damaged than its two commanders assumed when they started it moving under its own power again. Smith and Ismay should have waited another quarter hour or so while the man who supervised building the ship made a thorough damage inspection. Ismay was not noted for his patience.

Life in stokeholds aft of flooding Boiler Room #6 was dry but confused during the first ten minutes after the vessel struck on the iceberg. This confusion was the natural result of the accident and flooding. It was compounded by orders from the engine room which seemed to conflict with the damaged condition of the ship. Fireman Thomas "Paddy" Dillon was still struggling to shut the firebox dampers and draw the fires when the lights and bells on the Kilroy electric stoking indicators flashed and rang. The engine room was telling the black gang to "keep up the steam" despite obvious flooding. The men around Dillon shrugged and then began stoking the fires again.

Greaser [Frederick] Scott recalled the same unexpected orders in his testimony. Unlike Dillon, however, Scott's work placed him in contact with the ship's engines where he could see why it became necessary to keep up steam pressure in the dry boiler rooms. Scott remembered the engines rolling again at AHEAD SLOW for at least ten minutes. His memory was supported by Dillon who recalled the engines re-starting and then running for several minutes.

Quartermaster Olliver saw orders to re-start the engines sent down by the telegraphs from the bridge. "The *Titanic* went half speed ahead. The Captain telegraphed half speed ahead," Olliver testified to the U.S. Senate hearing. He did not recall if the engines were stopped at the time of that order, or if they were working slowly astern. He was certain *Titanic* was almost dead in the water when it started moving for the last time.

In the wheelhouse, Quartermaster [Robert] Hitchens must have been told to "steady up" on the ship's heading of just east of north. Otherwise, *Titanic* would have steamed in a giant circle with full right rudder given by Murdoch as he "ported around" the iceberg. Hitchens was kept at the wheel for more than 40 minutes after the accident, a job which would have accomplished nothing if the ship had not been moving. No amount of rudder movement has any effect on the heading of a stopped ship. Yet, Hitchens was kept at his usual post instead of being sent to help uncover lifeboats or fire distress rockets. The only logical reason

Hitchens remained at the wheel was to steer the ship after it resumed making way following the accident.

It has been suggested that Captain Smith resumed steaming in an attempt to reach the twinkling lights of *Californian*. If this had been true, Ismay would surely have claimed the ship sank itself during a desperate race to save the passengers' lives. Such a race would have transformed a blatant example of bad seamanship into a failed act of courage. Unfortunately, *Californian* does not appear to have been the destination. The small freighter had not been noticed from the crippled *Titanic* when the liner started moving again. Captain Smith was making for Halifax because it was the closest port for a large ship. The freighter just happened to be along the way.

Halifax was the only possible destination. In addition to being closer than New York, this Nova Scotia port had other attractions for Ismay. It was a major port with facilities that could be stretched to handle the sudden influx of people from the crippled liner. Rail connections would make it possible to get passengers to their final destinations. Also, Halifax was not a major city with a sophisticated network of reporters and wire services. In Halifax it would be much easier to control the flow of news about the ship than in the media center of New York.

Titanic's fatal decision made, the two men who commanded the ship parted company. Captain Smith left the bridge for the wireless office, a visit which opens another of the mysteries surrounding the sinking. It is most unusual that any captain would leave the command center of his damaged ship simply to "alert" the radio operators to a "possibility" that some message requesting help would be necessary. This was particularly true in 1912 when wireless was still considered more of a commercial novelty to amuse passengers than a useful tool. Preparing the operators for a possible eventuality was an errand too trivial for the Captain's personal attention. It should have been done by relief Quartermaster Olliver who would shortly return from his second errand of taking that note to Chief Engineer [Joseph] Bell. Sixth Officer [James] Moody was also on the bridge and could have been sent as he had no other pressing duties at that moment.

Smith must have had a compelling reason for making that trip personally. There is intriguing evidence that the

Captain's real motivation was to dictate a message to the White Star office in New York. It appears he wirelessed that *Titanic* had struck an iceberg; that everyone was safe; and they were steaming for Halifax. (All of this was true at 11:53 P.M.) Another ship from the Allen Line (probably *Virginian*) reportedly transcribed just such a message and forwarded it to the White Star office in Boston via a Canadian ground station. From Boston it went by land telegraph to the company's New York office.

Carpenter [John] Hutchinson rushed into the bridge enclosure only to find Captain Smith had departed for the Marconi room. His short conversation on the stairway with Fourth Officer Boxhall delayed him from reaching the Captain before the engines were re-started. There is no way to know for sure, but perhaps Hutchinson's report of the flooding mail room would have prevented Captain Smith from bowing to Ismay's demand to resume making way. Unfortunately, the engine room telegraphs were clanging while the Carpenter and Boxhall spoke on the stairway. By the time Hutchinson reached the bridge, the fatal mistake had been made and Captain Smith was on his way to the radio room.

Not Sinking?

While the Captain was visiting the Marconi office, Bruce Ismay went "down below" (his words) to confer with Chief Engineer Bell. Ismay knew the route to the engine rooms. He had visited Bell previously and allegedly had his own set of engineer's coveralls. His earlier visit had been to discuss the ship's speed and tonight's visit probably had a similar goal. Ismay appears to have been attempting to circumvent the Captain's authority again, if that could be done under the current circumstances. First he had to know the damage. Was the ship sound enough to increase speed, or to resume course for New York?

> MR. ISMAY: I asked if he [Bell] thought the ship was seriously damaged, and he said he thought she was. But [he] was satisfied the pumps would keep her afloat.
>
> U.S. Senate Hearings, April 19, 1912

Ismay's recollection of this short conversation may be the single most important piece of testimony given during either the British or American investigation. Without this particular information, the decision to re-start the ship's engines is unbelievable. Why would anyone try to steam for Halifax in a sinking ship? Ismay gives us the answer: *Titanic* wasn't sinking when the engines began beating again. According to Ismay, the Chief Engineer believed the pumps were effective against the flooding as late as 11:54 P.M. That was a dozen minutes after the accident. If Ismay was correct, Bell did not think the giant liner was foundering for several minutes after the engines began rolling again.

It is hard to imagine that an experienced engineer such as Bell would have overlooked something so important as his ship sinking. Accepting what Bell said at face value is much easier: *Titanic* was seriously wounded but not foundering almost fifteen minutes after the accident, even during the first few moments after it resumed making way. Put another way, it was not the ice that sank *Titanic*, but the actions of its captain and owner.

Bell had good reason for optimism during his conversation with Ismay. Almost immediately after the accident he had asked Captain Smith to release the watertight doors to allow his engineers to pass between Boiler Rooms #4 and #5 to rig a 10-inch suction hose. This door would not have been opened if Boiler Room #5 had been rapidly filling with water. Watertight doors are opened on a sinking ship only if compartments on either side of the bulkhead are thought safe from immediate flooding. . . . If the incoming water had been thought dangerous, the door to Boiler Room #4 would have remained tightly closed.

In any case, the British report said the new 10-inch line was enough to handle water spurting through the two feet of open seam in Boiler Room #5. More likely, however, this line was part of an apparently successful effort to slow the flooding in Boiler Room #6. The British report's claim of water eight feet deep at 11:51 P.M. is put into doubt by the Ismay/Smith decision to resume steaming. A flooded stokehold should have sufficiently alarmed even Bruce Ismay about the condition of the ship to delay making way again.

Confidence in the pumps that night was based on their performance during the quiet moments after the accident. Prior to steaming again at 11:50 P.M., *Titanic*'s pumps and bulkheads were doing a good job of controlling the flooding. Put simply, the ship was floating on its pumps. This was a precarious situation, to be sure, but far from the immediate disaster that ensued after Smith and Ismay resumed making way. Ten minutes after the ship started for Halifax, the pumps were being overwhelmed in Boiler Room #6. Once that happened, the system of watertight bulkheads was rendered meaningless. *Titanic* was condemned to a quick end.

What changed? Certainly not the pumps. If there was a change in the pumps, they would have become more effective as additional suction lines were connected. Surviving stokers and trimmers witnessed engineers rigging more lines to improve the discharge of water. As minutes ticked by, the pumping improved. This means that if the pumps were overwhelmed, there must have been an increase in the rate of flooding. The inescapable conclusion is that *Titanic*'s pumps were swamped by massive amounts of water pushed into the ship by its own forward motion. Water surged to eight feet deep in Boiler Room #6 within a few minutes of the engines turning again. *Titanic* appears to have steamed itself into a watery North Atlantic grave....

The End Comes

Even before its ill-fated maiden voyage, *Titanic* had captured the public's imagination. Everything about it was spectacular from its immense size to the sumptuous appointments of its two "millionaire's suites." In death, the ship lived up to the reputation it had created during its short life. The final moments were spectacular with the stern upended, pointing to the sky like the warning finger of a pagan sea god. There was the crashing sound of tearing metal prior to this final display, but that wasn't the sound most survivors remembered. As the taffrail disappeared, a great keening arose from those poor souls the ship had left behind. This wail continued until the last of more than 1,500 victims succumbed to the freezing water. Now, *Titanic* belonged not to the ages, but to the politicians, lawyers and tabloid journalists who would create great self-serving myths about the ship's demise.

One of those myths was that it sank intact, as perfect as the day it was launched. Thanks to Dr. [Robert] Ballard, we know the ship broke apart either at or near the surface just as witnesses in the lifeboats claimed. After breaking apart, Dr. Ballard's photographs show the two major sections (bow and stern) suffered far different fates. The bow planed away to the north with comparatively little damage caused by its plunge until it slammed into the bottom. The stern appears to have been heavily damaged by implosions as air-filled compartments were crushed as the section of hull plunged into the depths.

> *The inescapable conclusion is that* Titanic's *pumps were swamped by massive amounts of water pushed into the ship by its own forward motion. . . .* Titanic *appears to have steamed itself into a watery North Atlantic grave.*

Mostly because of testimony from the surviving officers, the myth grew that *Titanic* plunged intact to the murky depths of the Atlantic. The sounds of the ship tearing itself apart were ascribed to boilers exploding or falling through the bulkheads. "It sank in one piece," the myth proclaimed and nobody, not even eyewitnesses to the breakup, successfully challenged that version of the story for nearly 90 years. Survivors who witnessed the breakup and who described it in detail to investigators were simply ignored.

> After she got to a certain angle she exploded, broke in halve [sic], and it seemed to me as if all the engines and everything that was in the after part slid out into the forward part, and the after part came up right again, and as soon as it came up right, down it went again.
>
> —Frank Osman, Seaman, U.S. Senate Hearings, April 25, 1912

> She went down as far as the after funnel, and then there was a little roar, as though the engines had rushed forward, and she snapped in two, and the bow part went down and the after part came up and stayed up five minutes before it went down.

> She parted at the last, because the afterpart of her settled out of the water horizontally after the other part went down. First of all you could see her propellers and everything. Her rudder was clear out of the water. You could hear the rush of the machinery, and she parted in two, and the afterpart settled down again, and we thought the afterpart would float altogether.

Captain Smith Inadvertently Sank the Titanic

She uprighted herself for about five minutes, and then tipped over and disappeared.

—Edward John Buley, Seaman, U.S. Senate Hearings, April 25, 1912

. . . and she almost stood up perpendicular, and her lights went dim, and presently she broke clean in two, probably two-thirds of the length of the ship.

She broke, and the after part floated back. Then there was an explosion, and the aft part turned on end and sank.

—George Frederick Crowe, Steward, U.S. Senate Hearings, April 25, 1912

The tearing apart of the hull described in 1912 by these men, as well as other members of the crew and passengers, remains visible in the wreckage on the bottom today. There never should have been any doubt: *Titanic* broke apart either at or very near the surface of the sea and sank in pieces.

The amalgam of steel, wood and paint that had been the world's largest moving object began its descent to the bottom of the Atlantic Ocean at 2:20 A.M. on April 15, 1912. What rests there now is not *Titanic*, but the broken remnants of what was once a magnificent liner. Even as the real ship was disappearing into the dark waters, a new *Titanic* of myth and legend was being launched onto an ocean of public curiosity. It is this mythical ship, not the one of steel launched by Harland and Wolff [the *Titanic*'s builders], that still sails through the public imagination.

These two *Titanic*s share histories filled with mistakes, deliberate untruths and human errors. The real ship failed to follow the Rule of Good Seamanship with regard to lookout, speed, and prudence. The mythical one fails to follow the rules of physics with regard to turning, impact and even the method of flooding. And, while the two ships provide material for an unending stream of sea stories, the harsh reality is that the tragedy underlying them should not have occurred. Posting another lookout, choosing a more southerly course, reducing to a safe speed, or remaining stopped after the accident—any of these actions of ordinary seamen could have prevented the needless loss of life. But, history is not a record of what might have been.

For Further Research

Robert D. Ballard with Rick Archbold, *The Discovery of the Titanic*. Toronto: Madison Press, 1995.

Lawrence Beesley et al., *The Story of the Titanic, as Told by Its Survivors*. Ed. Jack Winocour. New York: Dover, 1960.

Steven Biel, *Down with the Old Canoe: A Cultural History of the Titanic Disaster*. New York: W.W. Norton, 1997.

Jennifer Carter and Joel Hirschhorn, *Titanic Adventure: One Woman's True Life Voyage Down to the Legendary Ocean Liner*. Far Hills, NJ: New Horizon Press, 1999.

John Dudman, *The Sinking of the Titanic*. New York: Bookwright Press, 1988.

John P. Eaton and Charles A. Haas, *Titanic: A Journey Through Time*. New York: W.W. Norton, 1999.

———, *Titanic, Destination Disaster: The Legends and the Reality*. New York: W.W. Norton, 1996.

Robin Gardiner, *The Titanic Conspiracy: Cover-ups and Mysteries of the World's Most Famous Sea Disaster*. New York: Carol, 1996.

Archibald Gracie, *Titanic: A Survivor's Story*. Chicago: Academy Chicago, 1998.

Walter Lord, *A Night to Remember*. Anstey, Leicestershire, UK: F.A. Thorpe, 1997.

———, *The Night Lives On*. New York: Morrow, 1986.

Donald Lynch, *Titanic: An Illustrated History*. New York: Hyperion, 1992.

Edward Eugene O'Donnell, *The Last Days of the Titanic: Photographs and Mementos of the Tragic Maiden Voyage*. Niwot, CO: Roberts Rinehart, 1997.

Charles R. Pellegrino, *Ghosts of the Titanic*. New York: William Morrow, 2000.

Index

Abelseth, Olaus, 116
accidents, 83
Adams, Stanley Herbert, 42
Adriatic (ship), 83
Almerian (ship), 65
Amerika (ship), 24
Andrews, Thomas, 10, 34, 93–94
  damage inspected by, 90
  response to iceberg collision, 97
Arabic (ship), 83
Astor, John Jacob, 96

Ballard, Robert, 98, 121
Baltic (ship), 31, 85
Barrett, Frederick, 109
Beesley, Lawrence, 11, 114–15
Birchfield (ship), 83
Blasco, Steve, 98–101
Boxhall, Joseph, 109
Brander, Roy, 88
Bride, Harold, 41–42
Brown, David G., 105
Buley, Edward John, 123

Californian (ship)
  book and film criticizing, 72
  Captain Lord's explanation defending, 64–66, 67–69
  crew on, 54
    recounting events to media, 58–59
  and distress signals, 13–14, 64–66, 76, 77
  ice warnings by, 31, 62, 96
  rescue efforts by, 65–66
  sighting *Titanic*, 55–56, 63–64
  unanswered questions regarding, 59–60
  wireless phone on, inability to hear *Titanic*, 56–57
Cannons, E.G., 44, 46
captains
  response of, to ice warnings, 44–45

  on *Titanic*'s rate of speed, 86
  of White Star Line, new instructions for, 50–51
  see also Lord, Stanley; Smith, Edward J.
Caronia (ship), 85
Carpathia (ship)
  and *Californian*, 57, 65–66
  news of *Titanic* disaster sent by, 18–20
  rescue efforts by, 14, 65–66
Charpy test, 100–101
Clarke, Maurice Henry, 92
coal, 82
Cox, Stephen, 13, 73
crew
  deaths of
    families affected by, 21–22
    number of, 10
  inability of, to handle lifeboats, 26–27
  negligence of, 47–49
  number of, 18
  saved by lifeboats, 14
  testimony by, as faulty, 109
  see also lookouts; Smith, Edward J.
Crowe, George Frederick, 123

Daily Telegraph (newspaper), 39
Davie, Michael, 80
Dillon, Thomas "Paddy," 117

Evans, Frank O., 56–57, 116
Everett, Marshall, 26

Ferguson, Duncan, 101, 102
Finlay, Robert, 75
fire, 27–28
Fleet, Frederic, 43, 96
Foweraker, A.M., 70

Gannon, Robert, 95

125

Garzke, William, 102, 113
Gibson, J., 54, 58
Great Eastern (ship), 90, 91
Groves, C.V., 53, 54, 57, 63
  sighting the *Titanic*, 55
  and wireless telephone, 59–60

Halifax, Nova Scotia, 118–19
Hampshire Chronicle (newspaper) 10, 17
Harrison, W.L.S., 72
Hesketh, James H., 109
Hitchens, Robert, 117–18
HMS *Hawke* (ship), 80–81

icebergs
  detection of, 40–43
  lookouts' sighting of, 96, 102
  as metamorphic rock, 87
  rate of speed among, 86–87
  short story on, 83–84
  sighted by *Californian* crew, 55–56, 63–64
  size of, 32
  visibility of, 31–32, 42, 44–46
  warnings on, 31, 84–85, 96
    by *Californian* crew, 62
    Captain Smith's response to, 47–49
    relaying to authorities, 41–42, 43
    responding to, 44–45, 46, 47
    and speed of ship, 49
    weighing risks of, 74
  see also Titanic, collision with iceberg
Ice Patrol, 86–87
Imax dive, 99
Ismay, J. Bruce, 10
  assessing damage, 119–20
  and ice warnings, 85
  interfering with ship management, 73–74
  on moving *Titanic* after collision, 116–17, 120–21
  and *Titanic*'s rate of speed, 23, 33–34, 85–86

KarisAllen, Ken, 101

Knapp, John J., 112

Last Log of the Titanic, The (Brown), 106
Latta, John, 71
Lee, Reginald Robinson, 42
Leyland Line. *See Californian*
lifeboats
  drills for, lack of, 26–27, 92–93
  lack of sufficient, 89, 91
  leaving half full, 92
  loading passengers onto, 11–12
  number of, 11
  passengers saved by, 14
Lightoller, Charles
  on Captain Smith's recklessness, 82
  on Captain Stanley Lord, 78
  on haze, 43
  on ice warnings, 43
  involved in previous collision, 81
  and lifeboat loading, 92
  responding to ice danger, 47, 48
lookouts
  detection of iceberg by, 40–43, 45–46
  failure of, to avoid iceberg, 13
  sighting of iceberg by, 96, 102
  see also crew
Lord, Stanley (captain), 61
  argument in defense of *Californian* by, 67–69, 72
  compared with *Carpathia* captain, 78
  controversy surrounding actions of, 13
  defending *Californian*, 72
  and disaster rockets, 77
  great care exercised by, 76–77
  inquiry of, 67
  letters and evidence in support of, 70–71
  new post of, 71–72, 77
  personality of, 54
  recounting events of *Titanic* disaster, 62–67
  removed from his post, 70, 77
  sighting ice, 55

Index

on sighting of the *Titanic*, 55, 56
  skepticism on actions by, 59
Lord, Walter, 89–90
Lowe, Harold, 87
Lusitania (ship), 83

Major, Albert, 26–27
Marcus, Geoffrey, 38
media, 17–20, 58–59
Mersey, Lord, 74, 75
Mesaba (ship), 85
Murdoch, William
  involved in previous collision, 81
  orders on dodging iceberg, 74–75, 106, 108, 109
  responding to ice danger, 48

National Maritime Museum, 99
New York Sun (newspaper), 23
New York Times (newspaper), 82–83
Night to Remember, A (Walter Lord), 72, 77–78
Nitrate Producers Steam Ship Co., 71, 77
Noordam (ship), 85

Oceanic Steam Navigation Company, 39
Olympic (ship), 34, 80–81, 82, 91
Osman, Frank, 122

Parisian (ship), 18
passengers
  deaths of, 10, 18, 20
  experiencing collision with iceberg, 11, 114–15, 116
  loading onto lifeboats, 11–12
  number of, 18
  realizing sinking of ship, 35
  rescue of, 14, 57–58, 65–66
  see also survivors

Reuter, Otto, 84
Rostron, Arthur, 78
Ryan, Patrick, 39
Ryan, Thomas, 39
Ryan v. Oceanic Steam Navigation Company, 39

Salem (ship), 20
Sanderson, Harold, 91
Scarrott, Joseph, 42
Scott, Frederick, 117
Shackleton, Ernest, 86
shipping companies
  competition among
    and breaking record for rate of speed, 85–86
    and captaincy, 82
  vs. meeting safety standards, 89–92
Smith, Edward J. (captain), 13
  and awareness of shipping accidents, 82–83
  and ice warnings, 44–45, 46, 85
  indifference of, to danger, 32–33
  involvement of, in previous collision, 80–81
  last dinner of, 34
  on moving *Titanic* after collision, 116–17, 118, 120–21
  negligence by, vs. weighing risks involved, 76
  ordering trip to Halifax, 118–19
  rate of speed under, 24–25, 85–86, 87
  response to iceberg collision, 97
  as a risk taker, 81–82
  was not advised by steamship manager, 73–74
Smith, William Alden, 12, 29
Southampton, England, 21–22
Stead, W.T., 58
steamships
  marine labor for, 36–37
  regulation of, 36
  see also shipping companies
Stewart, G.F., 54, 57, 59, 62
Stone, H., 54, 56, 58, 62
Stone, Mrs. George N., 26
Strachan, Frank, 71
Straus, Isidor, 96
survivors
  on crew's handling of lifeboats, 26
  number of, 18, 20
  relatives learning of, 19

see also passengers

Titanic
capturing public's imagination, 10–11
cost of suites on, 96
departure of, 81
at depths of ocean, 20
design of
and brittle steel, 101–102
meeting safety standards, 90, 91, 96
as watertight, 12, 34
disaster
blame for, 14
British Inquiry of, 38–39
decision on, 46–49
causes, 12–13, 89
captain's misplaced confidence, 24–25
indifference to danger, 32–33
lack of
ordinary care, 41–43
safety standards, 89–92
not detecting iceberg, 40–41
not hitting iceberg head-on, 74–75
responses
to iceberg, 45
to ice warnings, 47–49
steamship company competition, 89–92
as changing safety standards, 94
collision with iceberg, 96–97, 102–103
angle of, 102–103
crash stop was not used in avoiding, 109–10
felt as slight jarring, 11
head-on, 111–12
multiple impacts, 113–14
restarting engine after, 116–20
vs. running over the iceberg, 110–11, 114–16
side-swiping, 112–13
disaster signals sent during, 13–14, 64–65, 66, 76, 77
lessons learned from, 14–15, 104
media reports on, 17–20
passenger awareness of, 35
preventing, 13
public response to, 21–22
rate of speed prior to, 23–24, 33–35
among ice, 86–87
and breaking record, 85–86
real vs. mythological story of, 106
researching damage/tomb from, 98–99
short story paralleling, 83–84
sinking of ship, 97–98, 103–104
myths on, 121–23
unpreparedness for, 30–31
U.S. investigation on, 30
water entering ship, 34–35, 90, 97, 103
fire in, 27–28
route of, 11, 82
sighted by *Californian* crew, 55–56, 63–64
see also icebergs; lookouts; survivors
Touraine (ship), 85
transportation. *See* steamships

Virginian (ship), 18

White Star Line
captains of, new instructions for, 50–51
lawsuit against, 39
see also Titanic
Wilding, Edward, 112
Williams, Lord Justice Vaughan, 47
wireless telegraphy
on *Californian*, inability to hear *Titanic*, 56–57
during time of *Titanic* disaster, 85

LIBRARY
John Bowne High School
63-25 Main Street
Flushing, N.Y. 11367